THE ONLY
Basic Guitar
Instruction Book You'll Ever Need

Learn to Play—from Tuning Up to Strumming Your First Chords

Jack Wilkins and Peter Rubie

Adams Media
Avon, Massachusetts

Published by Adams Media, an F+W Publications Company, 57 Littlefield Street, Avon, MA 02322. U.S.A.
www.adamsmedia.com

ISBN: 1-59337-379-1
Printed in Canada.   J I H G F E D C B A

Library of Congress Cataloging-in-Publication Data available from publisher.

This publication is designed to provide accurate and authoritative information with regard to the subject matter covered. It is sold with the understanding that the publisher is not engaged in rendering legal, accounting, or other professional advice. If legal advice or other expert assistance is required, the services of a competent professional person should be sought.
—From a *Declaration of Principles* jointly adopted by a Committee of the American Bar Association and a Committee of Publishers and Associations

Many of the designations used by manufacturers and sellers to distinguish their products are claimed as trademarks. Where those designations appear in this book and Adams Media was aware of a trademark claim, the designations have been printed with initial capital letters.

Photographs courtesy of Peter Abréu. Illustrations by Barry Littman.

This book is available at quantity discounts for bulk purchases.
For information, please call 1-800-872-5627.

CONTENTS

Introduction

Introduction

A GUITAR can be many different things. It can be electric, or acoustic, or even electro-acoustic. It can be bluesy, classical, jazzy, folky, baroque, or just plain heavy. It can be big enough to fill a football stadium (if, say, Eric Clapton is playing it) or small enough to fill the circle around a campfire. A guitar can be loud enough to make your ears ring for hours afterward, or quiet enough to get a child to go to sleep.

In a similar way, an aspiring guitarist can be many people. He could be a beginning songwriter looking to get in touch with his inner poet, or maybe a longtime heavy metal fan trying to stay in touch with her inner headbanger. Someone may take up the guitar to play for her friends, or for that dreamed-of stadium crowd—or maybe just to play for himself, to prove that he could do it.

How then (you may ask), can this compact volume, *The Only Basic Guitar Instruction Book You'll Ever Need*, cover the many possibilities of this wondrous instrument, and help fulfill the varied goals of those people (yourself, for one) eager to play the guitar?

The answer is by carefully and thoroughly leading you through the basics, from "What kind of guitar should I get?" on up through "How do I play a blues progression?" In this book, you'll get all the guitar techniques, basic musical knowledge, and exercises and songs you need to progress from a beginner guitarist to an intermediate player who perhaps is on the way to even greater things.

Of course, this book itself is not enough to make you into an accomplished guitarist. There is that little matter of practicing (and more practicing . . . and more practicing). And you should look to find a guitar teacher you feel comfortable with who can help keep you on the right path and enable you to be the best guitarist you can be. Don't forget to look for advice from fellow guitarists. In becoming a guitarist, you're joining a community—a far-flung and widely divergent one, to be sure—of people who'd be happy to share their knowledge, and to help you along on the way to reaching your guitar-playing dreams.

one

Understanding the Basics, and Buying the Right Guitar

DID YOU EVER SEE those boxes in a discount store that say "My First Acoustic Guitar" or "My First Electric Guitar"? To tell the truth, one of those probably shouldn't be *your* first acoustic or electric guitar. You need to find a guitar that is of good enough quality to make the hours of practicing worthwhile, but not so expensive that it breaks your budget. In this chapter, besides learning the basic guitar facts and terminology, you'll find out all you need to know in order to find a guitar that is the right one for you.

The Anatomy of a Guitar

In order to read and understand the rest of this book, talk knowledgeably with a guitar salesperson, or take guitar lessons, there are a number of terms and words you'll need to be familiar with. The most basic vocabulary to master is this: What are all those different parts of a guitar called? That's what we'll talk about first. (By the way, a number of these terms, and other bits of musical jargon, are defined in the Glossary on page 139.)

If you look at **Figures 1-1 and 1-2**, you'll see that a guitar has three basic parts: a body, a neck, and a head.

Fig. 1-1: The parts of an acoustic guitar

Fig. 1-2: The parts of an electric guitar

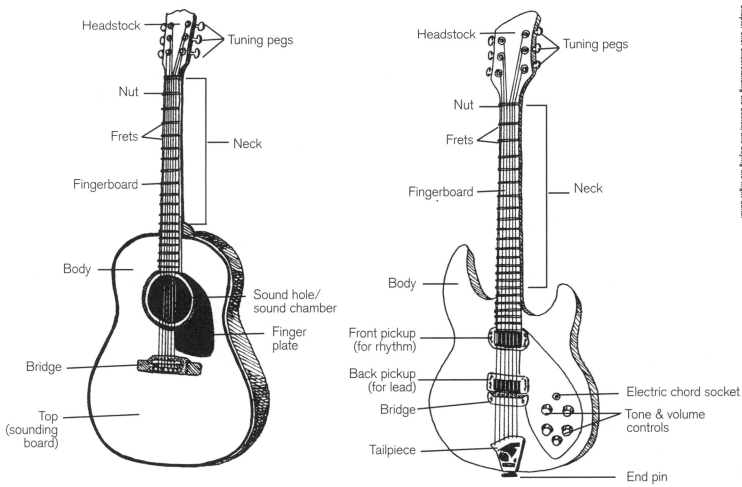

Fig. 1-1: The parts of an acoustic guitar — Headstock, Tuning pegs, Nut, Frets, Neck, Fingerboard, Body, Sound hole/sound chamber, Finger plate, Bridge, Top (sounding board)

Fig. 1-2: The parts of an electric guitar — Headstock, Tuning pegs, Nut, Frets, Neck, Fingerboard, Body, Front pickup (for rhythm), Back pickup (for lead), Bridge, Tailpiece, End pin, Electric chord socket, Tone & volume controls

The Body

The body in an acoustic guitar is where the sound comes from. It consists of a top piece, which is a sounding board with a sound hole, and a back and sides, which contain the sound and make it resonate.

In a purely electric guitar, the body is made of a solid piece of wood to avoid "feedback," or too much resonance or screeching when the sound is amplified. It also houses the electronic pickups (which convert the motion of the strings into an electronic signal that can be sent through an amplifier of some kind), and volume and tone controls (which vary the loudness and bass and treble frequencies of the signal). There is also a socket called an output jack, into which you insert a special plug or jack. The other end of the jack goes into a corresponding socket in an amplifier.

In addition, the body has a bridge, made from either wood or metal, which anchors the strings. There are also strap pins or posts, which you can use to attach a shoulder strap.

The Neck

The neck is usually fixed to the body by bolts or glue, or formed from the body in one piece. It often has a metal truss rod running through it to strengthen it and help adjust any slight warping or twisting. The neck has a flat piece of wood (usually mahogany or ebony) called the fingerboard or fretboard. The fingerboard is divided into sections called frets. These sections are marked off by pieces of wire set into the wood, called fretwire. By stopping a string in between the fretwires—that is, "in the middle of the fret"—the frets determine the different pitches or notes you can make on each string. The strings run from the bridge, along the neck and across the nut—which is a piece of wood, plastic, or metal at the top of the neck with slight grooves for each of the six strings—to the tuning pegs.

The Head

The head, sometimes called a headstock, holds the tuning pegs (also called tuning machines, machine heads, or tuning gears) that the strings are attached to. In a six-string guitar there are six tuning pegs. Each tuning peg has a knob you can turn using your fingers. The knob will tighten or loosen the string tension and thus put each string into "tune."

How Guitars Work

The principle of the guitar is simple. A string is stretched at high tension across the fingerboard between the tuning peg and either the bridge or the tailpiece. By using a fingertip to stop the string at various places on the fingerboard, and plucking the string near the sound hole, you can make the string produce a variety of pitches, or notes. The shorter the length of string, the higher the pitch; the longer the string, the lower the pitch. (That's why a double bass has a booming bass sound, and a mandolin or violin has a more high-pitched treble sound.)

String Thickness

There are three bass strings and three treble strings. (We'll talk a lot more about strings in the sections in Chapter 2 on tuning.)

As with string length, string thickness also affects pitch. The thinner the string, the higher the pitch. Besides the length of the string affecting whether you get a high note (short length = treble) or a low note (long length = bass) the strings range in thickness. The thinnest is the E String 1 (treble) and the thickest is the E String 6 (bass). The gauge of a string refers to its thickness. So you can have the same pitch on, say, the E String 1, but use different gauges.

By angling the bridge "just right" you change the string length and therefore help create the right pitch. You add to this by using strings of varying thickness called gauges, which are measured in millimeters.

Frets

Each fret on the guitar is a "half-step" away from the fret on either side. A half-step is the smallest interval, or distance between two notes, you can have in Western music. If you look carefully at a piano keyboard, you'll see it's mostly made up of alternating black notes and white notes that are half-steps away from each other.

On the guitar, to play two notes a half-step away from each other, all you have to do is stop any string in the middle of a fret, and then stop that string in the middle of the next fret. So to go up or down the guitar in half-steps, all you have to do is move your finger up or down the strings, stopping the strings one fret at a time.

Electric Guitars: Where Does the Sound Come From?

Electric guitars have added elements. Just like an acoustic guitar, shortening or lengthening a string will give you a variety of pitches, or notes. But without a hollow body that resonates, where does the sound come from?

The sound comes from electronic pickups, wire-wrapped magnets that act like tiny microphones placed under each string. The vibrations of the string cause the magnet in a pickup to resonate (or more accurately, to "modulate") a tiny magnetic field. That signal is picked up by the pickup and turned into a small electrical current. In turn, that current is conducted from the pickup to an external amplifier by an electrical cord that has one end plugged into the guitar and the other into an amplifier. How loud the note is—and whether it's distorted, or thick and bass-y, or thin and treble-y—is all determined by volume, tone, and effects controls on both the guitar and the amplifier.

Types of Guitars

There are three basic types of guitar to consider playing: classical; acoustic (and acoustic-electric) steel string; or solid-body electric. What you buy largely depends on the kind of music you want to learn to play.

If you're not sure exactly what you want to learn, or if you want to learn to play a number of styles, you should choose either a classical or a "folk" (acoustic) guitar. A classical guitar uses nylon strings, which are a little easier on your left-hand fingertips (assuming you're right-handed), though the neck is a little broader than a folk guitar. A folk guitar has steel strings, which are a little tougher on your fingertips at first, but it has a narrower neck.

Learning to play an acoustic instrument is cheaper and easier than going straight for an electric guitar and amplifier. Once you have some familiarity with the instrument, though, you'll know better which kind you want to learn to play next.

There are lots of different types of guitars built for the many different kinds of music you can play. To play Eric Clapton–like rock blues, you might buy a solid-bodied electric like the Fender Stratocaster or a Gibson Les Paul. For jazz guitar, you might consider an F-hole, hollow-bodied cello acoustic guitar like the Gibson ES-175 or a Gibson Super 400.

Blues and R&B guitarists often play a Gibson ES-335, or ES-355. To play folk music, like early Bob Dylan, go for a Martin or an Ovation. If you want to play classical or flamenco, start on a nylon-string guitar.

The truth is, though, that you can play anything on any kind of guitar. What counts is not the kind of guitar you have, but what's in your head.

Guitar Note

It might very well be the right thing for a first-time electric guitar buyer to buy a Squier Stratocaster or an Epiphone Les Paul copy instead of the name-brand "real thing." The difference in price is huge—a copy may cost on the order of $300 rather than $1,000—and the differences in quality and play are subtle.

Buying a Guitar: What to Look For

If you are relatively (or completely) inexperienced as a guitarist, the best thing you can bring along with you to a guitar shop is a friend who knows something about guitars and how to play them. If that's not possible, spend more time going to different stores, trying to learn as much as you can from different salespeople. Guitar magazines can also be a good source for information about the latest guitars and typical prices, though much of what they cover will not be as relevant to a beginning musician.

When you do go to a music store, the salesperson's first question for you will probably be "How much do you want to spend?" Know the answer ahead of time. Almost certainly, the next topic of conversation will involve what kind of music you want to play, and what level of technical accomplishment you've already reached.

Listen carefully to what the salesperson has to say, and don't be hustled into a sale. After the pitch, say that you'd like to think about it. Ideally, go to at least one other store and go through the process again. Listen for differences in what the two salespeople have to say to you about the same subjects. The following sections will tell you what to consider, evaluate, and ask about when buying a guitar.

Price

Buying a cheap guitar is usually not the best idea, though you don't have to spend thousands of dollars on an instrument and equipment, either. You should think in terms of at least $200 to $300. You could easily spend a $1,000 or more if you're not careful—especially if you get carried away with what you see in the guitar magazines.

Play a really expensive guitar (or have a friend or salesperson do so) and compare it to a much cheaper model.

What differences do you notice? Unless you are working as a musician and you're buying yourself a new tool of the trade, don't spend too much.

Used or New?
While a new guitar has to be broken in and can take up to six months to "wake up," a used guitar in good condition is "alive" and could be a bargain. You can expect to pay as much as 40 percent less than list price for a used guitar (unless it's a classic of some sort), depending on where you get it. Compare the prices in music stores, secondhand stores, and newspaper ads, and gather as much knowledge and information as you can.

Construction
Gently tap the top and back of the instrument to make sure nothing rattles. (You're listening for loose struts inside.) Look inside the sound hole for glue spills and other signs of sloppy workmanship. Check that all the pieces of wood join together smoothly and that there are no gaps between pieces.

An acoustic guitar's sound is principally made by the top—the back and sides reflect and amplify the sound. So a solid-wood acoustic guitar is preferable to a laminated-wood guitar (where the manufacturer presses together layers of inexpensive wood and covers the top layer with veneer). However, solid-wood guitars can be very expensive, and laminated-wood guitars can be pretty good. They are sometimes stronger than solid-wood guitars; the lamination process results in a stronger (though less acoustically responsive) wood.

With electric guitars, make sure that knobs, wires, and other metal parts are secure and rattle-free. Strum the open strings strongly and listen for rattles. A solid-body guitar is basically an electric instrument with no real acoustic sound. The wood that it's made from is irrelevant. It is all electronics. So make sure the pickups and wiring are in good working order. There should be no hum or shorts, and the volume and tone controls should all work without crackles or other noises.

Another important consideration is how long the note will sustain. To check this out you need to use an amplifier for best results. Fret a note and play it. Don't use an open string and don't move the string; just keep fretting the note until it fades away. A good sustain period is four seconds or more, which means the guitar will be good for playing fusion and rock. It also means the guitar is in good order. If the sustain is less than four seconds, then it's a questionable instrument and you should think twice about buying it.

Neck

Pick up the guitar by the head and peer down the neck to make sure it's not warped. Does the guitar have a truss rod? Most guitars now come with them, but make sure. Does the neck bolt on? You can usually see where the neck is attached at the heel with a heel plate, under which are four or five bolts. Fender Stratocasters and Telecasters have bolt-on necks. Is the neck glued on? Classical guitars, or the Gibson Les Paul, have glued necks. It looks as though the neck and the body are made from one piece of wood.

Run your fingers along the edge of the neck to make sure the fret wire doesn't need filing or reseating. The fret wire should be seated well on the fingerboard, and the ends should not be loose or feel jagged. Is the neck made from ebony, rosewood, or maple? Cheaper guitars use mahogany or plywood stained black or rust red. The more expensive guitars with the better fingerboards are worth the money. Are the notes at the bottom of the neck in tune? Are they as easy to play as the notes at the top of the fingerboard? Do any of the notes have a buzzing sound even though you're stopping them properly? Is the intonation accurate? Do the notes on the twelfth fret correspond to the harmonics at the same place? The notes may have different tonal qualities, but they should have the right pitch. Pay attention to the third and sixth strings in particular. On a guitar that's not set up well, or has a problem, these strings may be hard to keep in tune.

𝄞 Guitar Note

Is it a good idea to buy a guitar through mail order or over the Internet? Not really. Just like buying a car, you need to "test-drive" the instrument, making sure that you're comfortable with it and that it works. Just knowing the make and model isn't a guarantee that a particular instrument is worth buying, or worth the money people are asking for it.

If you don't trust your own knowledge or ears, enlist the help of an experienced guitarist. It's vital to make sure you don't buy something that's going to be really hard to play.

Action

The instrument's "action" or playability is determined by the setting of the string over and between the bridge (at the bottom of the guitar) and the nut (just before the tuning heads). The strings shouldn't be so low that the notes buzz when they are played, nor so high that the notes need a lot of physical strength to hold down. If the notes are hard to play or out of tune, get someone in the store to adjust the instrument. If they can't (or won't) fix the instrument, don't buy it.

Before You Buy

Here are a few more things to check before you put down your credit card to purchase your new guitar:

Check the fingerboard for warping—Look down the neck as if sighting down a rifle barrel. It's normal to see slight curving around the seventh fret, which can be adjusted using the truss rod, but if the neck looks twisted, don't buy it.

Check the intonation—The twelfth fret should always be exactly one octave higher than the open string.

Check the tuning heads—If they turn too easily the strings may slip, making the guitar difficult to keep in tune.

For an electric guitar, check the pickups—Make sure each string has the same volume level. Significant differences can indicate the pole (or screw beneath each string) may need to be adjusted. If not, the whole pickup may need replacing.

Check for noise—With the guitar plugged in, stand it close to an amplifier and listen. Whistling or feedback might suggest the pickups aren't well isolated, and it could be a problem playing the guitar at high volume. Make sure the amplifier in the store is not masking faults with the guitar you're playing.

A Few Words about Practicing

Now that you either own a guitar or are ready to buy one, let's say a few things about something that's even more important than the quality of your guitar—the amount, and the quality, of the practice time you put into learning to play the guitar.

You have to be honest with yourself about how much time you can put into practicing. Ideally, your practice time and place should be the same every day. You should practice in a well-lit area with a comfortable chair and a music stand.

Write out a schedule for yourself and stick to it. It is essential that you practice in a relaxed manner. If you strain, you'll run the risk of muscle problems with your shoulders or your hands. Take lots of breaks during your practice session, partly to relax and to rest your muscles, and partly to ensure that you don't build in mistakes into your playing technique in an attempt to "get to the next stage" as quickly as possible.

If your hands start to tighten or cramp, stop and take deep breaths or a short walk, which will ease the tension and calm you down at the same time. You will actually improve much faster if you allow your hands and fingers to develop slowly and at their own speed.

You will need to develop a practice schedule that works best for you. No matter what your schedule or level of commitment, try to be consistent.

You should try to spend five or ten minutes every day on the same thing. Repetition breeds a familiarity, which creates a confidence that will help you on to the next stage. This can become tedious and boring, however, so you have to strike a balance between maintaining your interest and perfecting your skills. If you can't do something every day, try to do it two or three times a week. Again, the keys are repetition and consistency.

two

Tuning and Maintaining Your Guitar

NO MATTER HOW GOOD YOUR GUITAR IS, it's not going to make a good sound unless you tune it right and care for it properly. Changing the strings regularly is also essential for keeping your guitar in the right playing condition.

The Standard "Concert" Tuning

There are lots of ways of tuning your guitar, and lots of types of tunings you can experiment with. For now we're going to concentrate on only one tuning—the standard "concert" tuning. The thickest bass note is called String 6, and the strings are tuned as follows:

String 6: E
String 5: A
String 4: D
String 3: G
String 2: B
String 1: E

Notice that the top string (1) and the bottom string (6) are the same note, but two octaves apart.

Strings 6, 5, and 4 are the bass strings. Strings 3, 2, and 1 are the treble strings. String 6 is the thickest. String 1 is the thinnest.

Try to memorize the names of the open strings. Once again, they are E, A, D, G, B, and E. Make up a phrase starting with each letter so you can easily recall the string names.

Fig. 2-1:
Open strings and notes on the 5th fret

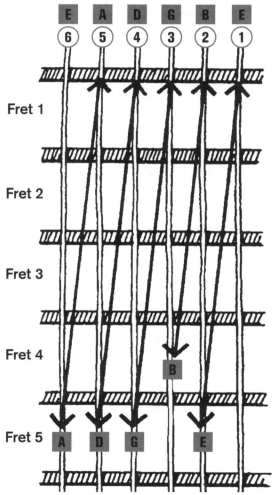

Fig. 2-2:
The open guitar string notes on a keyboard

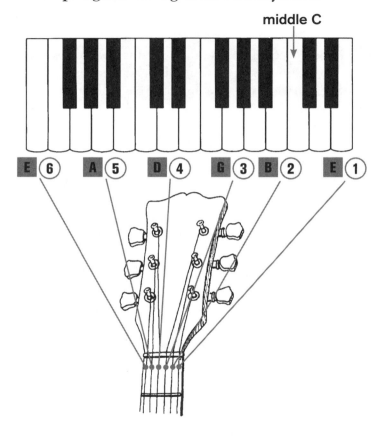

Relative Tuning

The easiest way to tune your guitar if you're playing alone is called *relative tuning*. That means the guitar is in tune relative to itself, although not necessarily to other instruments. You can tune the guitar from any string, but usually you start from String 6, the E bass string.

To begin, count up five frets—that is, five spaces between the fret wires (see **Figure 2-1**—on String 6. Then use your first fingertip on your left hand to stop the string at this fret and play the note. This is the note A. Now play String 5 while the note on String 6 is still sounding. (Make sure to play String 5 "open"—that is, without stopping it at any frets.) Listen for the "wow-wow-wow" sound the two strings make as they sound together. Is the note of String 5 higher or lower than the note of String 6? If it is higher, then you are sharp. Turn the tuning peg on String 5 to lower the sound of the note. If it is higher, then you are flat. Turn the tuning peg until the note sounds higher.

Keep playing both strings at the same time, or one string immediately after the other, so that both notes are sounding at the same time. If you're not sure, keep lowering the note on the open string until it is obviously too low, then try raising it again. The closer you get to being in tune, the more the "wow-wow-wow" sound will slow down and eventually disappear. When it disappears completely, you're in tune. Just get it as close as you can for the moment.

Next, stop String 5 at the fifth fret and play the note there. (The note is D.) Play String 4 open at the same time. Again, adjust the open string using the tuning peg until both strings are sounding the same note.

Next, stop String 4 at the fifth fret and play the note there (G). Play String 3 open at the same time. Again, adjust the open string using the tuning peg until both strings are sounding the same note.

Notice that tuning String 2 is slightly different. Stop String 3 at the fourth fret and play the note there (B). Play String 2 open at the same time. Again, adjust the open string using the tuning peg until both strings are sounding the same note.

Next, stop String 2 at the fifth fret and play the note there (E). Play String 1 open at the same time. Again, adjust the open string using the tuning peg until both strings are sounding the same note.

If the strings are new, they may slip a little bit. Tuning is about constant adjustment. So don't be afraid to go back and try to adjust the strings already in tune to make sure they haven't gone out of tune a little bit.

Other Ways to Tune a Guitar

Here are some other things you can do to make sure the strings are in tune with each other:

Play String 1 and String 6 together—They're both E strings, remember (though two octaves apart). Try to make sure they sound like the same note.

Play notes an octave apart—To do this, stop String 5 at the seventh fret. This sounds the note E. Now play String 6 (E) open at the same time. Make the adjustment to the higher-pitched, fretted string. The two notes are an octave apart. Do the same on the other strings. Remember, on String 3 stop the string at the eighth fret and play String 2 open to sound the note B. Then play the String 2 at the seventh fret and String 1 open.

Match octaves by playing every other string—Again, make the adjustment to the higher-pitched, fretted string. Play String 6 (E) open, then stop String 4 at the second fret (E) and sound that note at the same time. Then match String 5 (A) open with String 3 stopped at the second fret. Play String 4 (D) open, with String 2 stopped at the third fret. Play String 3 (G) open with String 1 stopped at the third fret.

Tuning Using Harmonics

Harmonics is a complicated subject, and this method of tuning is one you may want to take a look at again after you've gained more experience. For now, just accept the following. If you lightly touch a string over the fret wire on the twelfth fret with a finger while gently plucking close to the bridge, you will get a note called a *harmonic.*

Following the same "light touch" technique, play the harmonic on String 6 at the fifth fret (E), followed by the harmonic on String 5 at the seventh fret. Adjust String 5 until it's in tune.

Compare harmonics on String 5, fifth fret (A), and then String 4, seventh fret. Adjust String 4 if necessary.

Compare harmonics on String 4, fifth fret (D) with String 3, seventh fret. Adjust String 3.

Compare harmonics on String 6, seventh fret (B) with String 2, twelfth fret. Adjust String 2.

Compare harmonics on String 5, seventh fret (E) with String 1, twelfth fret. Adjust String 1.

Strum a chord, such as G, A minor, or E, one string at a time (arpeggio style), and then together, and listen to the strings working in harmony with each other. Bear in mind that a string may sound out of tune in one chord, and work well in another.

Types of Strings

Strings come in a variety of gauges. The thicknesses are described in fractions of an inch. In general, the lighter the string gauge the easier it is to bend and hold down the strings for lead playing. The thicker the gauge, the better the volume, the longer the sustain, and the easier it is to keep the guitar in tune. A thicker gauge is also easier for rhythm playing. The common gauges are:

Ultra-light:	.008 (String 1) to .038 (String 6)
Extra-light:	.010 (String 1) to .050 (String 6)
Light:	.011 (String 1) to .052 (String 6)
Medium:	.013 (String 1) to .056 (String 6)
Heavy:	.014 (String 1) to .060 (String 6)

Strings come in three different types: nylon, usually for Spanish or classical-style guitars; bronze, used for acoustic steel-strung instruments because they have little electrical quality; and steel strings, used for electric and acoustic instruments. You should never put steel or bronze strings on guitars that use nylon strings. It will ruin them quickly.

With the exception of Strings 1 and 2 (and sometimes also 3), which are plain metal, steel strings are made up of a thread or core of wire around which another piece of wire is tightly wound. There are three types of winding:

- *Flatwound.* Most commonly used on archtop guitars, a flat ribbon of steel is wound around a core of wire. Flatwound strings don't "squeak" the way other strings can when you move your fingers along them, but they can produce a somewhat duller tone and are more likely to crack.

- *Roundwound.* Most electric steel strings are roundwound, a piece of steel that is wound around a steel core. They have a brighter tone than flatwound, and often last longer, but seem a little tougher to play at first.
- *Groundwound.* These are conventional roundwound strings that have been ground down to create a partially flat surface.

🎼 Guitar Note

Being able to tune the guitar to itself is great, but what if you're playing with other musicians and your guitar is out of tune with them? You tune to a fixed source. You can use pitch pipes, a tuning fork, a piano, another guitar, or an electronic tuning box to help you put each string into "concert" pitch. (This is the term for commonly accepted pitches that everyone uses, regardless of their instrument.) You can even find music software programs that will give you the correct pitch for your strings.

Changing Strings

Depending on how much you play, and whether you live in a hot climate or not, you may need to change your strings as often as once a week. In general, though, once every eight to twelve weeks is about average. If a string breaks, it's probably time to change the whole set, rather than just replace the one that broke. Strings lose their stretch and vibrancy over time because of salt from sweaty fingers and rust.

It has been said that replacing strings one at a time is better for the guitar because it maintains tension on the neck. Not true. However, replacing strings one at a time can be more convenient.

A potential problem with taking all the strings off at the same time is that on guitars with a movable bridge, the bridge will move. Resituating a bridge can be a pain, and if it is not positioned properly, it can effect the tuning of the strings and the feel of the neck as you play. A good compromise is to replace the strings three at a time. Replace the bass strings first, putting them in rough tune with the old treble strings, and then replace the treble strings, putting them in tune with the new bass strings. Then you can adjust the tuning of all six new strings.

You can just unwind the strings by lessening the tension using the tuning peg, or you can try a more radical approach and use wire cutters to snip the strings near the tuning peg. Once the old strings are off the guitar, throw them away.

Classical Guitars

Classical guitars have fixed bridges, so you can replace the strings all at once if you like. Nylon isn't as springy as steel, but attaching the string to the bridge can be tricky at first.

Figs. 2-3a and 2-3b: Attaching nylon strings to a bridge

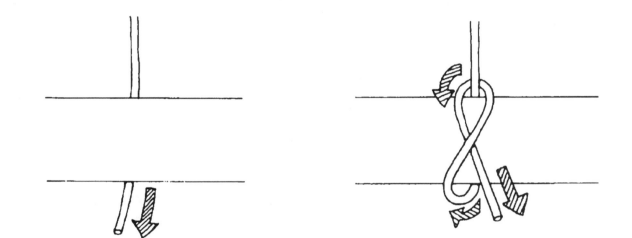

Guitar Note

You can extend the life of your strings by cleaning them after each session. To get rid of the grunge under the string, some players "snap" each string by pulling it back slightly, as if the string is on a bow, and then snapping it back to the fingerboard.

Fig. 2-4: Nylon strings attached to a bridge

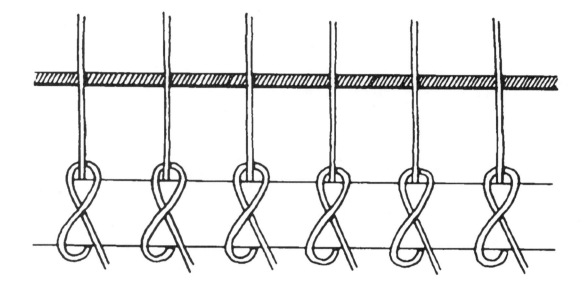

Fig. 2-5: Attaching strings to a tuning peg

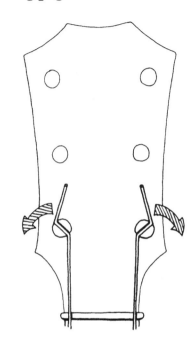

**The arrow indicates the direction
to turn the tuning peg**

Pass the string through the hole in the bridge, leaving about an inch and a half sticking out the back. Loop the short end back up, and wrap it behind the long end and then under itself. Pull it taut by tugging on the long end of the string. You may have to practice this a few times. Don't cut the string until everything is in place and in tune.

Fig. 2-6: Order of strings as they are attached to the tuning pegs

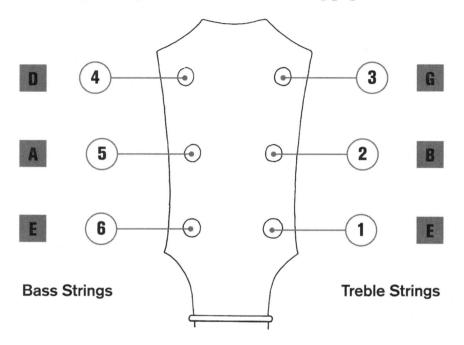

Bass Strings   Treble Strings

Thread the long end through the hole in the tuning peg at the head. (**Figure 2-6** shows the order of the strings on the head.) Bring the end of the string over the roller (or capstan) in front of the hole and under itself. Make sure the string sits in the small groove on the nut. Then take up some of the slack of the string and tighten the tuning peg by winding the bass strings from right to left (counterclockwise), and treble strings from left to right (clockwise). As it picks up the slack of the string, the tuning peg will tighten and lock itself in place. While the string tightens, start tuning it and stretching it by pulling on it at various times. Once the guitar string is in place and in tune, snip away the excess string, leaving maybe a couple of inches at the tuning peg, and an inch or less at the bridge.

Steel-Strung Acoustic Guitars

Steel-strung acoustic and electric guitars have a moveable bridge, so when you change the strings you want to be careful not to dislodge it. It's a good idea to change the strings one at a time, or three at a time, but not all at the same time in order to keep the bridge anchored in its best position.

Acoustic guitars often have bridges that anchor the end of the string by popping the string into a hole and keeping it in place with a pin. First, loosen the string by slackening off the tension at the tuning peg. Then ease out the bridge pin.

Bridge pins can stick sometimes, so carefully use needle-nose pliers or the blunt edge of a table knife to ease the pin out of its hole. Be careful not to dig into the wood. Once the pin is out, you can remove the string.

Stuff the end of the new string that has a little brass ring into the bridge pin hole. Then wedge the bridge pin back into the hole, locking the ring and the string in place. You'll notice that the pin has a slot. Make sure the slot faces forward (i.e., toward the tuning pegs).

Now pass the string over the bridge post, making sure each string fits snugly into the groove on the bridge and on the nut. Thread the loose end through the hole in the tuning peg post. If you want, you can kink the string a little to help keep it in place. Take up the slack on the string and then turn the tuning peg clockwise for the treble strings, and counterclockwise for the bass strings, tuning the string as the tension increases.

After all the strings are attached, retune the guitar carefully, bringing all the strings up to concert pitch. Be careful; you don't want to break a string. The best technique is to turn the tuning peg a couple of times, then check the tuning until you get the string in tune. When the string is in tune, clip the end off at the tuning peg, leaving about an inch of extra wire protruding.

Electric Guitars

With electric guitars, the string is attached to the bridge by passing one end through a hole and threading the string up to the brass ball, which keeps it in place.

Some guitars use what is called a locking nut system, such as a Floyd Rose tremolo unit. These can be a pain to change. The strings are clamped into place at the bridge saddle using a special Allen key. It's a good idea to use a piece of wood or a pack of playing cards to take up the tension when a string is changed; this stops the unit from rocking back and forth. On tremolo units, when one string is changed, the tension on all the strings changes.

In order to use these bridges, you must snip off the ball so that the string can be fitted into a small vise-like mechanism that holds the string in place. When all the strings are changed, you can remove the wood or playing cards supporting the bridge. Tune the strings as usual, using the tuning pegs. Then make the final adjustment on the bridge anchor using an Allen key. But be careful. Don't overtighten the strings at the bridge too soon. If you overtighten a string, when you remove the block supporting the unit, the string may snap as the tension increases.

Remember, if you have a guitar with this kind of bridge, the spare strings need to have the ball ends removed. Get in the habit of carrying wire cutters around in your guitar case.

Cleaning and Caring for Your Guitar

As with many things in life, the simplest way to maintain your guitar is this: Clean it. If dust gathers under the head and bridge, dust them off by using a cloth or feather duster, which can clean without the danger of scratching.

Natural oils from your fingers coat the strings every time you play. Over time the strings start to corrode, which can damage the strings' ability to sound good and also eventually injure the wood of the instrument. Wipe down the guitar after every playing session and before you put the guitar back in its case—front, sides, back, fingerboard, and back of the neck as well. A chamois leather cloth not only cleans but polishes at the same time.

Use a cloth to clean each string. Hold the cloth between your thumb and index fingers, and then run them along the length of each string.

If the guitar has not been used for a while, first dust it and then rub down the wood with furniture polish or, better yet, guitar polish. (Some types of furniture polish contain abrasives that can damage the guitar's finish.) Never put polish directly onto the instrument; it can damage the finish. Put your cleaning solution onto a cloth first.

For the metal parts, you may want to use a mild jewelers' or chrome polish, so long as it's not abrasive. Be careful! Don't ever touch the pickups of an electric guitar with anything besides a dry brush or cloth. Pickups are electrical, and liquid can cause a short-circuit. Avoid keeping your guitar in a place that's subjected to direct sunlight for long periods of time, or drastic changes in temperature and humidity. This will help keep the guitar surface from cracking. If you do accidentally chip the surface, take the guitar to a professional guitar repairperson, who will easily fix the problem. If you decide to do it yourself, bear in mind that when you add or remove varnish, it can drastically change the wood's ability to vibrate, and thus the guitar's sound.

Adjustments and Minor Repairs

If you're often unhappy with how your instrument plays or sounds, it's usually a good idea to take your guitar to a repair professional for possible alterations and adjustments. Here are some adjustments an experienced repairperson or player (and as you grow more confident in your knowledge, you yourself) can make.

Adjusting the Bridge

By adjusting the bridge you can alter the action of your guitar. The action describes the height of the strings above the fingerboard. The higher the action, the more strength you need to use to fret a note. It can be useful for rhythm playing, when you are principally playing chords all the time. Blues players who use "slides" often use a high action so the "bottleneck" doesn't scrape against the frets.

The lower the action, the easier it is to fret the note. This can be useful for fast, single-note lead guitar playing. Ideally, you want to set the action as low as you can without getting fret buzzing.

Adjusting the Neck

Temperature changes, humidity, and age can cause guitars to swell and contract. This in turn can affect the setup of the guitar. For example, a slight bow in the neck can cause fret buzz, or difficulty getting a clean note at a particular fret or series of frets. You can sometimes adjust the neck by manipulating the truss rod. (The truss rod runs down the center of the neck just under the fingerboard. Not all guitars have them, and even some that do won't allow you to adjust them.) But if you can't fix the problem within a few turns, stop. Overtightening or overloosening the truss rod can ruin a guitar and make it permanently unplayable.

Loose Connections

If you hear a rattle, try strumming the instrument and touching various potential culprits with your free hand until you touch the correct object and the rattling stops. For example, it could be a loose screw in a tuning peg or a loose nut on a jack socket. It's a good idea to gather a small toolkit of screwdrivers, pliers, wrenches, and such that will fit the various sizes of screws and nuts on your guitar.

Tuning Pegs

Tuning pegs, tuning machines, or machine heads (different names for the same thing) are easily replaced if gears get worn or a part breaks off. If more than one tuning peg is giving you trouble, it's probably a good idea to replace the whole set.

The tuning pegs screw into the wood of the head, so take off the string, unscrew the tuning peg, take the peg to a guitar store, and try to get a matching peg. Then screw the new peg into place in the same position as before.

Strap Pins

These are little buttons that you use to attach a strap to the guitar. They usually have regular screw bodies, and they can sometimes work themselves loose. If tightening the pin with a screwdriver doesn't work, dab a little plastic wood or carpenter's glue on the end and put it back. If you still have trouble, go to a professional.

Electric Problems

Dust and other grunge can affect the electrics of your guitar. If your volume or tone controls start to crackle when you turn them, or you're getting a weak or inconsistent signal, you may have dust or something else on the control. Turn the knobs vigorously back and forth to see if you can work out the dirt. If that doesn't work, try spraying the controls inside with aimed blasts from a can of air. If all else fails, go to a professional, who will give your controls a thorough cleaning.

three

Holding the Guitar, and Understanding Written Music

NOW THAT YOU'VE GOT THE RIGHT GUITAR, and know how to take care of it, there are just two more things to learn before getting to the fun part (playing it!). One is the correct way to hold the guitar and strum it, either with your fingertips or a pick. The other thing to become familiar with in this chapter is how music is written for the guitar.

The Right Position: Sitting and Standing

Before you start playing, you need to be able to comfortably cradle the guitar so that you're relaxed when you play. There are a number of ways of doing this. Let's begin with sitting.

The traditional position for playing classical guitar is to raise the neck of the guitar to about 45 degrees from the vertical; in this way, the head of the instrument is about level with your shoulder, while the "waist" of the guitar rests on your left thigh. Placing your left foot on an adjustable footstool can help maintain this position. By holding the neck at this angle, you get the maximum positioning of your left hand on the fretboard, and your right hand over the strings. The hands do not support the neck in this position.

Fig. 3-1: Classical pose   **Fig. 3-2: Informal sitting pose**

The more informal seated position is to rest the waist of the guitar on your right thigh, while the inside of your right arm holds the body of the instrument in place, and your left hand gives slight support to the neck.

30

If you decide to play standing up, make sure you buy a good strap that will comfortably support the weight of the guitar and not cut into your shoulder at the same time.

Fig. 3-3: Standing

The guitar should hang comfortably against your body, leaving both your arms free. If the strap is adjusted properly, the neck of the guitar should be at about a 45-degree angle. The bridge should be about level with your waist, and the head about level with your shoulder.

Left-Hand Position

The best way to fret a note cleanly is to exert the maximum pressure using your fingertips. To do this, you need to develop a good left-hand technique. First, let the edge of the neck of the guitar rest in the palm of your left hand. You'll notice that your thumb and fingers automatically fall to either side of the neck. Now place the left-hand thumb in the middle of the back of the neck so that there is a nice space between the neck and your palm. You should be able to pivot your whole hand on the ball of your thumb without banging into the neck.

Fig. 3-4:
Placing the thumb in the middle of the back of the neck

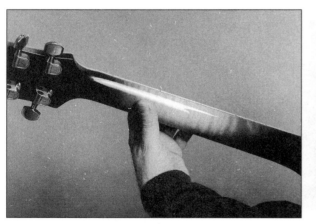

Fig. 3-5:
Holding the string against the fret with the fingertip pad

Guitar Note

If you have a solid-bodied electric guitar, the seated position can be awkward because the weight of the head and neck will dip down, making the guitar hard to play. You'll need to use a shoulder strap.

When you fret a note, use the tip or pad of your finger to press the note firmly to the fingerboard. If you put your thumb immediately behind the place where you're pressing the string to the fretboard (as if you're trying to pinch thumb and finger together through the neck), you'll get maximum pressure on the note and it will sound clean.

Figs. 3-6 and 3-7: Left-hand position

Try the following exercise: Place the tip of your first finger on the first string at the first fret, as shown in **Figure 3-8**. Now pluck the string with your right-hand thumb.

Fig. 3-8

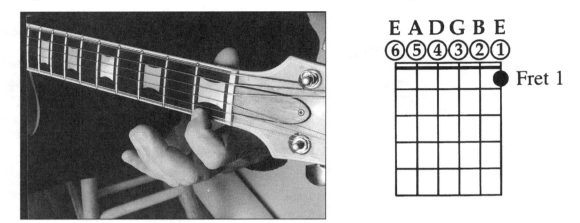

Fig. 3-9

E A D G B E
⑥⑤④③②①

● Fret 1

Take a look at **Figure 3.9**, which represents what you've just done. Each vertical line represents a string, and each horizontal line represents a fretwire. The double line at the top represents the guitar nut. The black dot or number represents the finger you should use to stop that string at that fret—in this case, at the note F on the first string.

Press the string to the fretboard roughly in the middle of the fret (between the fretwires). If you press too close to a fretwire, the string may be muted; too far away and the string may buzz. To make sure you don't mute other strings, make a point of using your fingertips and keeping your fingers as vertical as possible to the strings by arching your wrist slightly.

A lot of players let their left-hand thumb come over the top of the neck. They even use it to fret bass notes. This is perfectly fine, but it's hard for beginners to do. Remember, the more your hand is cramped up like this, the harder it is to play the note well and the more your muscles may ache.

Right-Hand Position

The right hand can be used *fingerstyle*, which means that each finger of the right hand manipulates the strings (as in classical or folk/blues fingerpicking styles). You can instead hold a plectrum or pick in your right hand to strum various rhythms or pick out notes on the strings.

Fingerstyle

The basic fingerstyle position is to use the fingernails to pluck the strings. (At first, you may use your fingertips as well.) The fingers are held vertical to the strings with a slight arch in the wrist. The thumb plays the three bass strings, while the first finger plucks the third string, the second finger the second string, and the third finger the first string; the little finger is not usually used.

Fig. 3-10: Right-hand position

For now, just practice strumming all six strings first with a pick, and then using just your thumb. The key is to place your fingertips on the fingerplate to anchor your hand, and then brush your thumb across all the strings. You'll learn about more complex techniques later in the book.

How to Hold a Pick

The size and thickness of a plectrum, or pick, can vary; as a beginner, you'll want one of medium size and thickness. Let the pick lie flat on your first finger, and then comfortably hold it in place with your thumb. You can then use it to strum the string with up-and-down motions. The movement should come from your wrist, not your fingers.

Fig. 3-11: Holding a pick

Fig. 3-12: Strumming with a pick

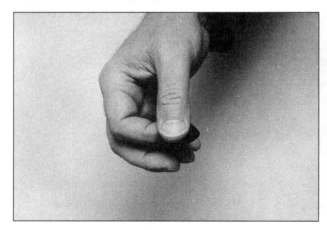

To get an idea of the proper strumming motion, take your right hand and extend the fingers, thumb and first finger lightly touching at the tip. Now, with the fingertips still touching, shake your hand up and down at the wrist in a gentle, comfortable motion.

♪ Guitar Note

When you're beginning to play the guitar, as soon as your hand or fingers get sore or start to hurt, stop! It will take a little time for the strength in your fingers to build up. Playing a little bit often is better than playing a lot in one go.

Writing Music as Chords and Slashes

There are three basic ways to write down music for the guitar. The first way uses chord symbols and slashes, which represent the number of times you should strum a chord. Each slash represents one down stroke or strum of a chord.

Fig. 3-13: Using chord symbols and slashes to write music

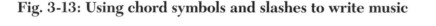

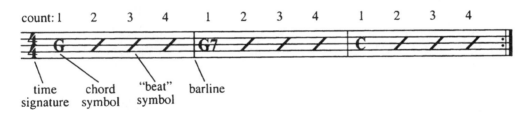

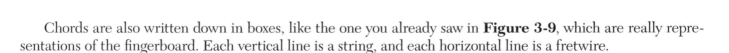

Chords are also written down in boxes, like the one you already saw in **Figure 3-9**, which are really representations of the fingerboard. Each vertical line is a string, and each horizontal line is a fretwire.

Fig. 3-14: The chord diagram for E (Major)

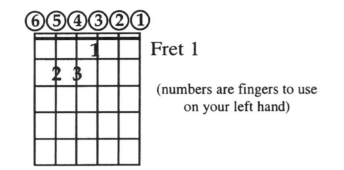

Fret 1

(numbers are fingers to use
on your left hand)

Each circle or number represents a place where you should put your finger on the fretboard and the finger you should use to stop the note. The name of the chord is usually written under the diagram.

Look at the chord diagram, and you'll see that the chord has a distinctive "shape." Let's call this one the "E" shape. Each finger has a certain place it should be on the fingerboard in order to play the E chord. If you move your fingers over a string (i.e., the chord shape starts not on the String 5 but on the String 4), then the "E" shape will make the chord "A minor." It's a good idea to think about chords as "shapes" that can be moved around the fingerboard. This will be very useful later on (really!). The fingers are numbered as shown in **Figure 3-15**.

Fig. 3-15: The fingers of the hand, numbered

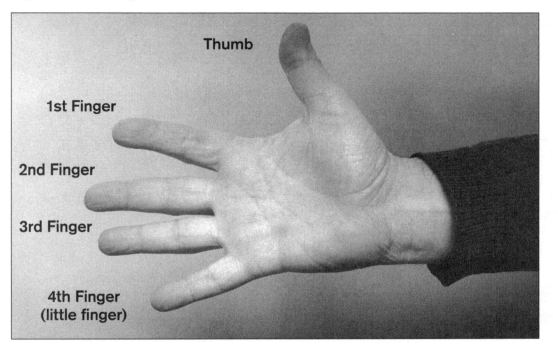

Guitar Tablature

Another way to write down music is using guitar tablature. Here, each line represents a string on the guitar, with the top line the first string, and the bottom line the sixth string. The numbers on each line represent the fret you need to stop in order to get a note. You can show complex fingerings this way, including chords, and melodies.

Fig. 3-16: Guitar tablature

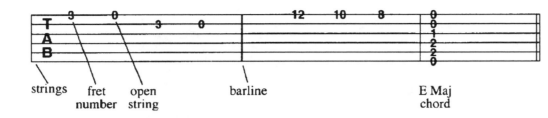

strings   fret   open   barline   E Maj
        number   string   chord

Standard Notation

The third method for writing guitar music is standard notation, the common method of written music you are already at least a little familiar with. This looks a lot like tablature, except instead of six lines there are only five.

Fig. 3-17: Standard notation

In Chapter 6, we'll talk a lot more about how to read music. But first, in Chapters 4 and 5, we'll talk more about chords and—this is why you're here—we'll start to play a few songs.

 **four**

**Playing Your First
Songs and Chords**

AS PROMISED at the end of the last chapter, you're now going to learn to strum some songs. To do this, you'll need to learn a few chords. A *chord* is made when three or more strings are played together, usually by strumming down with a pick or plectrum, or by using your thumb. Let's get playing!

Chords C and G7

The first chords you'll learn here are easy versions of fuller open string chords you'll learn later. Their names are C and G7. Try to memorize the names of the chords and the shapes they make.

Figs. 4-1a and 4-1b: Playing the chord C (major)

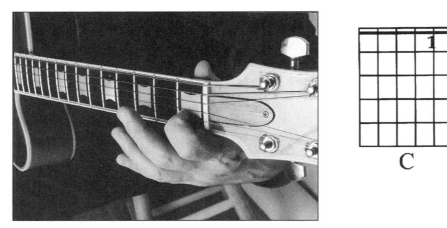

To play the chord C (major), put your first finger on the second string at the first fret. Press hard. Strum Strings 1, 2, and 3 together four times. You've now strummed four beats. When it is written this way, it is a bar of music: | C / / / |

42

Figs. 4-2a and 4-2b: Playing the chord G7

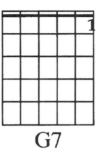

G7

Strum the chord four more times. You've now strummed two bars of C. (| C / / / | C / / / |)

To play the chord G7, put your first finger on the first string at the first fret. Play the first three strings again, strumming four times.

Play the C chord four more times. And then another four times. Play G7 four times. Now play C four times.

If that sounds familiar, it's because you've just played the song "Merrily We Roll Along." This is how it looks in chord slash style:

Merrily We Roll Along

4/4 C / / / | C / / / | G7 / / / | C / / / |
     C / / / | C / / / | G7 / / / | C / / / ||
Merrily we roll along, roll along, roll along,
Merrily we roll along, over the deep blue sea.

The 4/4 at the beginning means count and play four beats in every bar. If it was 3/4 at the beginning, you would play and count three beats in the bar. The bars are created by bar lines that look like this: " | " It is usual to write four bars per line and then go to another line. In "Merrily . . ." for example, the first bar is C for four beats, and the second bar is also C for four beats. The third bar is G7 for four beats, and the fourth bar is C for four beats. The next line is a repeat of the first line, so that the song has a total of eight bars altogether.

Next, try this tune:

Go Tell Aunt Rhodie

4/4 C / / / | C / / / | G7 / / / | C / / / |
    C / / / | C / / / | G7 / / / | C / / / ||

Go tell Aunt Rhodie, go tell Aunt Rhodie,
Go tell Aunt Rhodie, the old grey goose is dead.

Chords D7 and G

The next chord is D7, which uses three fingers. Study the chord chart: Third finger on second fret of first string; first finger on first fret of second string; second finger on second fret of third string.

Figs. 4-3a and 4-3b: D7

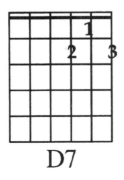

D7

Figs. 4-4a and 4-4b: G

G

This chord is going to take some practice before it sounds clear. A good exercise is to try to press hard and play the chord. Then relax your hand but keep the shape of the chord made by the fingers, raise them off the guitar strings, and then put the shape back on the strings—again, pressing hard. This can help build "muscle memory," so that the fingers remember where they should go to form this chord.

Guitar Note

Right about now, you may find that your fingertips get sore. And as you change chords, it's a challenge to jump your finger smoothly from the first string to the second string and back again. The trick is to practice slowly and try to aim for good technique. Slightly arch your wrist, use your fingertips, and press firmly with your thumb in the middle of the back of the neck as you press down with your fingertip to stop the string. Try to eliminate all sounds of buzzing. Keep your other fingers out of the way.

The next chord is the full open-string version of the chord of G. If you have trouble with this, just play the note on the first string and strum the first four open strings.

Twinkle Twinkle Little Star

4/4 G / / / | C / G / | C / G / | D7 / G/ |
    G / C / | G/ D7/ | G/ C / | G/ D7/ |
    G / / / | C/ G/ | C/ G/ | D7 / G/ ‖

Twinkle twinkle little star, how I wonder where you are
Up above the world so high, like a diamond in the sky,
Twinkle twinkle little star, how I wonder where you are.

In this song, in the second and third bars and elsewhere, you'll play two beats of C and then two beats of G. This is a hard tune to play, so practice it a lot until you get comfortable changing.

This next tune, "Amazing Grace," has a *key signature* of 3/4. This means you strum three beats to the bar. Notice also that the second bar is blank. This means that you should repeat the previous bar. So bar two would be another three beats of G, as would be bar six. Bar eight will be three beats of D7, etc.

Amazing Grace

3/4 G / / | | C / / | G / / |
    G / / | | D7 / / | |
    G / / | | C / / | G / / |
    G / / | D7 / / | G / / | ‖

Fuller Versions of Chords

Try these fuller versions of the chords C and G7, and then go back and practice these songs using the full versions.

Figs. 4-5a and 4-5b: A fuller version of C

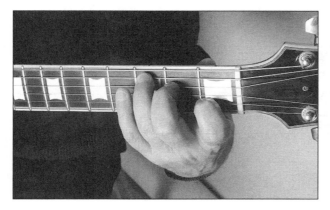

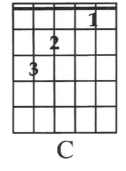

C

Figs. 4-6a and 4-6b: A fuller version of G7

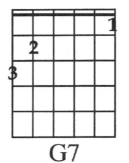

G7

Four Songs to Play

The following are the full versions of some of the songs noted in this chapter. Use the tablature if necessary.

Fig. 4-7: Merrily We Roll Along

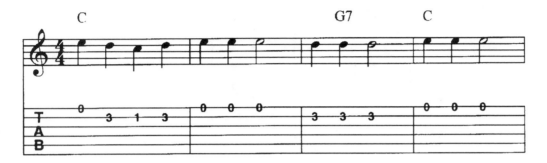

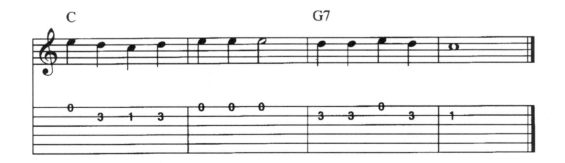

Fig. 4-8: Go Tell Aunt Rhodie

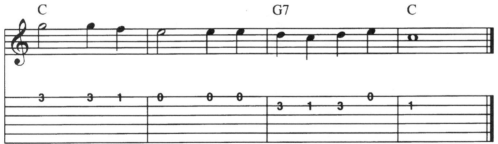

Fig. 4-9: Amazing Grace

(count: 1 2 3)

(hold & count: 1   2   3   1   2)

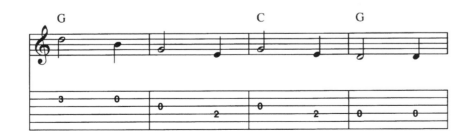

Fig. 4-9: Amazing Grace continued

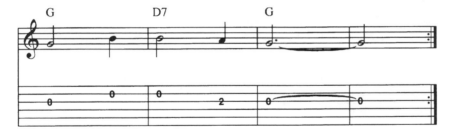

Fig. 4-10: Twinkle, Twinkle Little Star

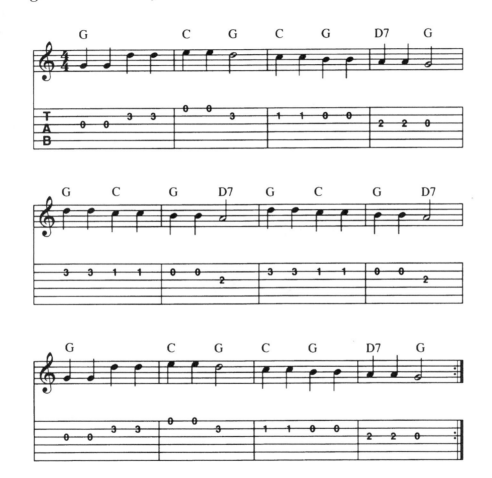

five

**Picking and
More Open-String
Chords**

YOU SHOULD KEEP WORKING on the chords you've already learned to play (practice, practice!). In learning to play the guitar (as with any instrument), you have to continually reinforce and improve what you already know. But right now, let's look at some right-hand things you can study, and add some chords to your repertoire.

Right-Hand Picking

Holding and using a pick is a bit more complicated than just brushing the strings with your thumb. If you haven't done it already, play the songs in Chapter 4 using your thumb the first time through, and then the pick the next time through.

There are two distinct ways of hitting the string with a pick: a *downstroke* and an *upstroke*. To make a downstroke, use the tip of the pick and push down.

Upstrokes are the reverse. The tip of the pick is used to pull up on the string.

To master using a pick, you need to become very comfortable mixing downstrokes and upstrokes. This is the only way to get any kind of speed and articulation in your playing.

Figure 5-1 contains some exercises to help develop right-hand picking. They use open strings and are written in both music notation and tablature.

Fig. 5-1: Right-hand picking exercises

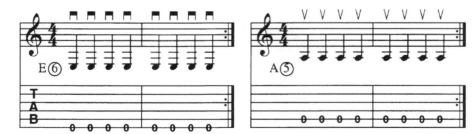

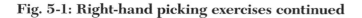

Fig. 5-1: Right-hand picking exercises continued

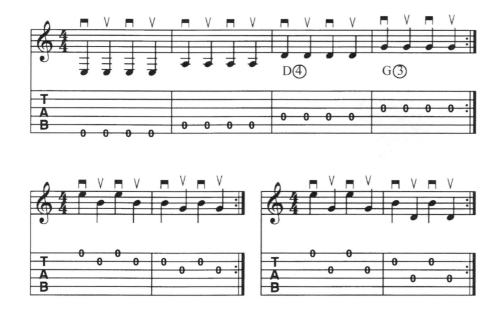

♪ Guitar Note

Doing the exercises in **Figure 5-1** will be a lot more complicated if you're left-handed because you'll need a left-handed guitar. If you get one, then just do everything in a mirror image, substituting left hand for right hand and vice versa.

Minor Chords

Let's try a new type of chord. It's called a *minor chord*, and it has a sad or bluesy quality to it. Minor chords are written with a capital letter followed by a small *mi*; we'll show you three of them: Ami, Emi, and Dmi.

Figs. 5-2a and 5-2b: Ami

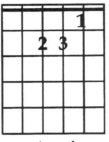

Ami

Figs. 5-3a and 5-3b: Emi

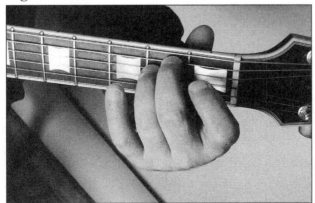

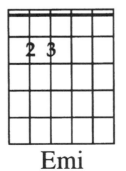

Emi

Figs. 5-4a and 5-4b: Dmi

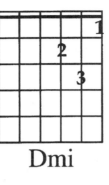

Dmi

Here are three songs that use minor chords. Note: In the last two songs, the first word of the song is in parentheses at the beginning so you know where you are starting.

Drunken Sailor

4/4 Dmi / / / | | C / / / | |
    Dmi / / / | | C / / / | Dmi / / / ||

What shall we do with the drunken sailor?
What shall we do with the drunken sailor?
What shall we do with the drunken sailor?
Earl-eye in the morning
Wey, Hey and up she rises,
Wey, Hey and up she rises,
Wey, Hey and up she rises,
Earl-eye in the morning

Swing Low, Sweet Chariot

4/4 (Swing) ‖ D / / / | G / D / | G / D / | Emi / A / |
                  D / / / | G / D | D / A / | D / / /   ‖

Auld Lang Syne

4/4 (Should) ‖ G / / / | D / / / | G / / / | C / / / |
                   G / / / | D / / / | Emi / Ami D | G / / / ‖
                   G / / / | D / / / | G / / / | C / / / |
                   G / / / | D / / / | Emi / Ami D | G / / / ‖

Chord Families

Chords go together in families (or, as they are formally called, *keys*). For example, a G7 chord is part of the C family, and a D7 chord is part of the G family. Play those chords and they just seem to fit naturally together. A D7 chord, for example, does not lead to a C chord nearly as well as it leads to a G chord. Try it and see.

Chords break down into three basic types:

Major chords (like G or C), which sound happy.
Minor chords (like Ami and Dmi), which sound sad.
Dominant seventh chords (like G7 or D7), which sound slightly jazzy and seem to want to lead us to resolve to a major chord.

Let's take a look at three more chords. These are part of the key (family) of A: A, D, and E7.

Figs. 5-5a and 5-5b: E7

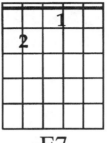

E7

Figs. 5-6a and 5-6b: A

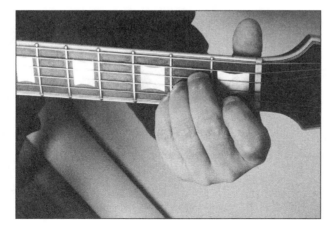

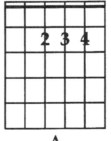

A

Figs. 5-7a and 5-7b: D

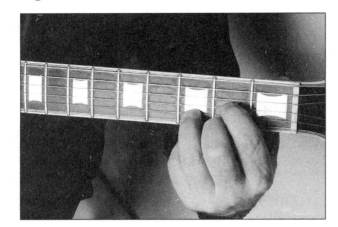

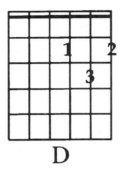

D

Yankee Doodle

4/4 D / / / | D / A / | D / / / | D / A /|
    D / / / | G / / / |A / / / | D / / / ||

Kumbaya

4/4 (Kum-ba-) || A / / / | / / D / |A / / / | |
                A / / / | / / D/ | E7 / / / / | |
                A / / / | / / D/ |A / / / |/ / D / |
                A / / / | / / E7 / |A / / / | ||

When Johnny Comes Marching Home

```
3/4  (When)|| Ami // |          |          |          |
             Emi // |          |          |          |
             Ami // |          |          |          |
             C //   |          |          |          |
             Ami // |          | Dmi // |          |
             Ami // |          | E7 // |          |
             Ami // | E7 //  | Ami // |E7 // |
             Ami // |          |          |          ||
```

Open-String Chords

The following groups of chord diagrams contain all the open-string chords you should learn. One of the things that makes learning chords easier is that families (keys) share the same chords, or variations on them. So once you know how to play a C chord, or an E7 chord, it will be the same regardless of the sequence you find it in.

Fig. 5-8: Open-string chords

Key (family) of G

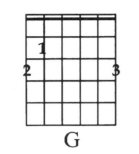
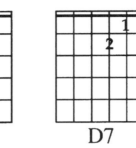
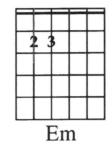

G   C   D7   Em

Key of A

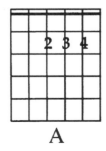
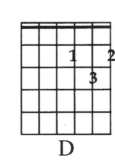
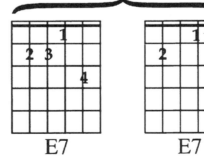

A   D   E7   E7

(alternate fingering)

Fig. 5-8: Open-string chords continued

Key of C

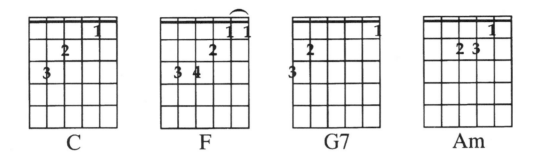

C   F   G7   Am

Key of D

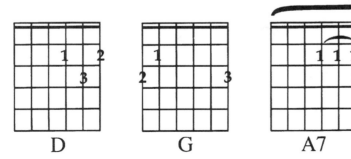

D   G   A7

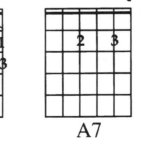

A7

(alternate fingering)

Fig. 5-8: Open-string chords continued

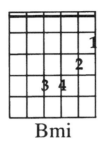

Bmi

Key of E

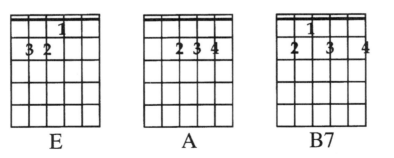

E   A   B7

Fig. 5-8: Open-string chords continued

Key of F

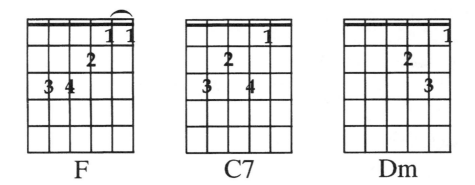

F C7 Dm

Guitar Note

With your knowledge of these chord families, you can now buy some song books, or look on the Web for some song sheets you can download. Make sure they have the chords to the tunes printed on them so you can practice the songs.

Practicing Chords

Spend some time working on changing smoothly from one chord to another as you strum. Some of these chords involve using your first finger to stop more than one string. To do this, use the fatty part of your finger. Initially, you may want to lay your second finger on top of your first finger to help you make just enough contact with the strings on the fretboard so they don't buzz.

If you pay attention, you'll notice some chords in the same key are missing. That's because they can't be played with open strings. You will soon learn how to play these chords.

Left-Hand Fingering

Notice in **Figures 5-9a and 5-9b** how each finger of the left hand should play a particular fret. The first finger plays the first fret, second finger plays the second fret, third finger plays the third fret, and the fourth or little finger plays the fourth fret.

Figure 5-10 is a left-hand fingering exercise. You should play this using each finger to a fret, with the first finger on the first fret, second finger on the second fret, and so on. (Normally, you would not play the "B" on the fourth fret third string, and the open second string. But for the purposes of this exercise go ahead and do it anyway.)

Figs. 5-9a and 5-9b: Left hand fingering exercise

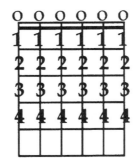

Fig. 5-10: Each finger to a fret

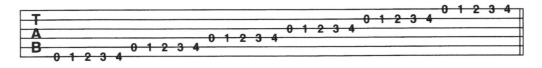

Three Practice Songs

To end this chapter, here are some extra songs you probably recognize and which you can practice using what you've learned so far.

Fig. 5-11: Jingle Bells

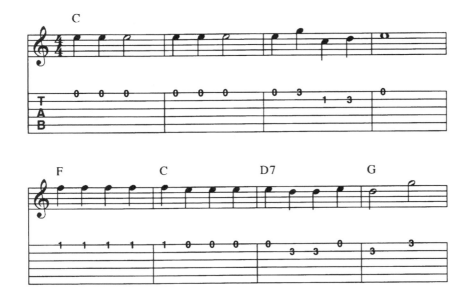

Fig. 5-11: Jingle Bells continued

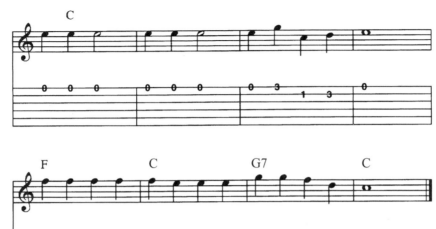

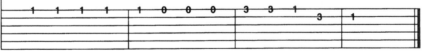

Fig. 5-12: Simple Blues in E

Fig. 5-13: **Simple Minor Blues**

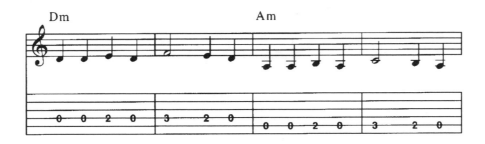

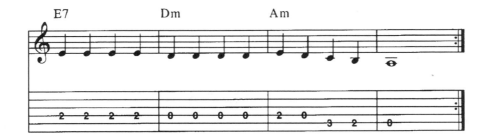

 six

The Basics
of Reading Music

IF YOU'VE EVER HAD A BASIC MUSIC CLASS, some of what follows in this chapter will be familiar. You will learn something new here, though: how this basic music theory relates to playing the guitar. What you learn now will give you a good foundation for the more advanced techniques and concepts in the rest of the book.

Rhythm and Tempo

Having a good knowledge of "where the beat is" and playing in time are essential for a musician. Time breaks down into two elements: rhythm, or the "feel" of a piece of music; and tempo, or the speed you play at. Music often has a suggested tempo marking on it that may look like this: ♩ = 120. The number 120 refers to the number of beats per minute (bpm) on a metronome. It denotes how fast (or slow) the piece should be played. The lower the number, the slower the piece of music. The higher the number, the faster the piece of music. In general, these are the accepted tempos in music:

Grave: very slow, slower than 40 bpm
Lento: slow, 40 to 60 bpm
Adagio: slow (at ease), 60 to 75 bpm
Andante: walking, 75 to 100 bpm
Moderato: moderate speed, 100 to 120 bpm
Allegro: fast (cheerful), 120 to 160 bpm
Vivace: lively, 150 to 170 bpm
Presto: very fast, 170 to 200 bpm
Prestissimo: as fast as possible, 200 or more bpm

Written Music in Standard Notation

When you write out music in tablature, as shown in Figure 6-1, you have a problem.

Fig. 6-1: Music in tablature

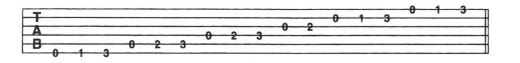

The problem is, we can't easily use this kind of chart to show how long we should sound a note. One beat? Two beats? Three beats? How can you tell?

To solve that problem, we split the note up so that it lasts for different lengths of time—all of which are reflections of each other.

Whole note: = 4 beats

Half note: = 2 beats

Quarter note: = 1 beat

Eighth note: = ½ beat

Sixteenth note: = ¼ beat

Time Signatures

As you've seen, we write 4/4 at the front of a piece (or sometimes 3/4, and so on). The top number (4 or 3) tells us how many beats in the bar to count. The bottom number tells us the kind of note we are counting (in this case, a quarter note). So if 4/4 means four quarter notes to each bar, and 3/4 means three quarter notes per bar, then 2/2—also known as common time—would be two half notes to the bar. What would 6/8 be? Six eighth notes to the bar. And so on.

The notes in the bar have to add up to whatever the time signature says. For example, 3/4 would mean the notes must add up to three. Then a bar line | is drawn, and we start the next group of three. If the notes had to add up to four, then we would make sure there was a bar line every time the notes added up to four.

For example, the following quantities of notes each add up to four beats:

one whole note   eight eighth notes
two half notes   sixteen sixteenths
four quarter notes

The following groups each add up to three beats:

one half note and a quarter note
three quarter notes
six eighth notes
twelve sixteenth notes

Rests, Dotted Notes, and Tied Notes

What if you don't want a note to be played? Each of the notes has a corresponding rest note, which indicates that you should not play for that brief period. So you could also make up beats by inserting a half note and a quarter note rest, or a half note rest and a quarter note, or two quarter notes and a quarter note rest, and so forth. See **Figure 6-2**.

Fig. 6-2: Rests

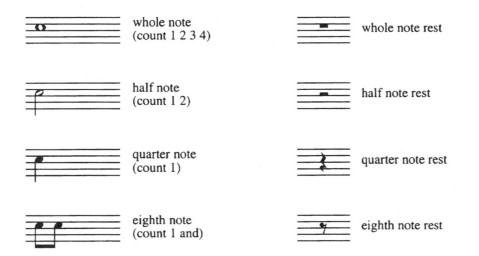

whole note
(count 1 2 3 4)

whole note rest

half note
(count 1 2)

half note rest

quarter note
(count 1)

quarter note rest

eighth note
(count 1 and)

eighth note rest

If we write a dot immediately after a note, it will increase that note's duration by half as much again. For example, a dotted whole note would be four beats plus two, totaling six. A dotted half note would be two beats plus one, totaling three. A dotted quarter note would be one beat plus a half of a beat. (In this case, the next note would start on the "offbeat.")

Another way to make a note last longer is to tie two notes together. In **Figure 6-3** for example, you play the first note, keep your finger down and continue to count for the length of the second note that is tied to the first with a curved bar connecting the two notes.

Fig. 6-3: Tied notes

count 1 (2   3)   1   2   3   (1 2 3)

Basic Musical Notation

There are only seven notes in the musical alphabet, and then they repeat themselves: C-D-E-F-G-A-B (then C again, which is considered an "octave" or eight notes higher than the first C you played). You can start the sequence on any note you like, but it still repeats after 7 notes. (For example, A-B-C-D-E-F-G-[A]; F-G-A-B-C-D-E-[F], etc.)

There are two basic elements to reading and writing music: the name of the note in the musical alphabet; and how long that note should last. Over time, these two elements became combined into one elegant system—called *musical notation.*

The modern staff is split into two halves, each of which is called a clef, and each of which has a particular sign at the beginning to tell us which staff we are using. These clefs are called the *treble clef* and the *bass clef.* When piano players read music, they play the treble clef with their right hand and the bass clef with their left hand.

Notes that appear below or above the clefs appear on what are called *ledger lines*—individual lines for each note. Look at **Figure 6-4**. In between the treble clef and the bass clef is one note on a ledger line. That note is called middle C because it is the note C and it falls in the middle of the two clefs. It is usually played on the guitar as the note on String 5, third fret.

Fig. 6-4: Middle C

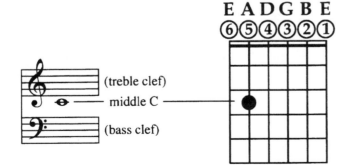

Because the notes on the lines and the spaces make up the musical alphabet in sequence, the note on the space after middle C will be D. The note on the next line will be E, on the next space F, and so on.

Finding Notes on the Guitar

The great thing about the guitar is that you only have to learn the notes on the treble clef. If we look at all the notes on the lines, beginning with middle C, we see that they are:

Fig. 6-5

The notes on the spaces above middle C are:

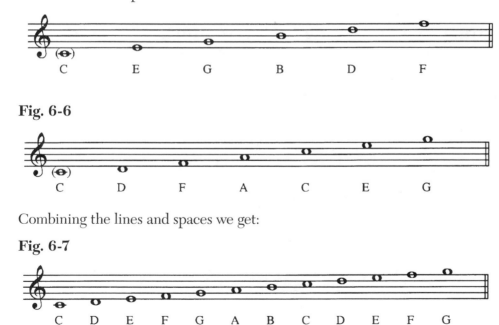

Fig. 6-6

Combining the lines and spaces we get:

Fig. 6-7

This is quite simple if you are playing the piano. However, a little problem arises when it comes to playing the guitar. You may have noticed when you practice tuning up that you can play the same note (as it appears on the treble clef) in different places on the guitar. E, on the top space, for example, can be played on String 2, fifth fret, or on String 1, open. The solution to the problem (developed by the great guitarist Segovia) is that, above the notes, you indicate the string you should use.

Now we just need to find out where these notes are on the guitar. Here are some exercises on the open strings that have fingerings to help you learn the musical alphabet.

Fig. 6-8

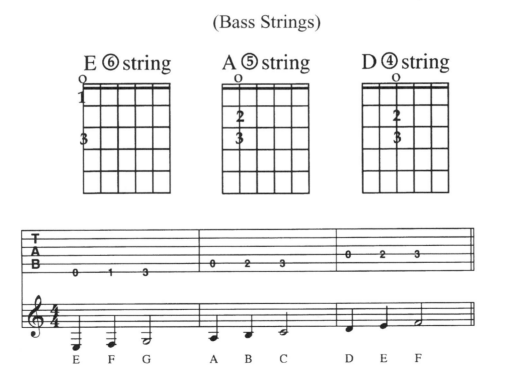

Fig. 6-9

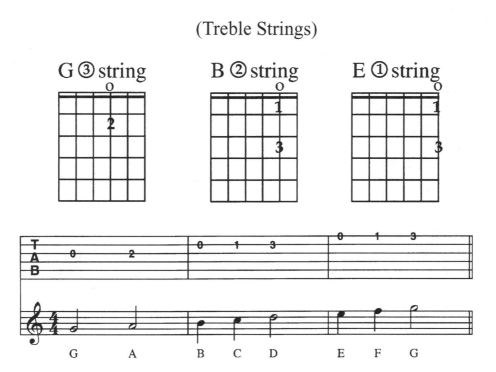

(Treble Strings)

G ③ string   B ② string   E ① string

Go back to some of the songs in the last two lessons and try reading the music now.

Dynamic Markings

Dynamics basically concerns how loud or how soft you play the note or the chord. As with the tempo indications, the dynamic markings in music have Italian names. Here they are with their symbols:

pp: pianissimo, very quietly
p: piano, quiet
mp: mezzo piano, moderately quiet
mf: mezzo forte, moderately loud
f: forte, loud
ff: fortissimo, very loud

Key Signatures

Notes can be on lines (E-G-B-D) or spaces (D-F-A-C-E-G) on the staff, and we can raise or lower these notes using sharp (#) and flat (♭) signs. *Key signatures* allow us to put these sharps or flats at the beginning of a piece of music; this tells us that all the notes on that line or space in the piece should be played as though they have a sharp or flat sign in front of them. The exceptions are when a natural sign (♮) tells you to not play a particular note flat or sharp.

Depending on how many sharps or flats there are at the beginning of a piece of music, we can tell which key the music is written in. Here are the main key signatures you need to know:

🎼 Guitar Note

Staccato means "short and sharp." When you play staccato, you keep the rhythm of the piece, but you play the notes for a shorter duration than you normally would. Staccato notes are often marked with dots underneath. The opposite of staccato is *legato*, which means "slurred." Here you slur the notes together, maybe playing one note and hammering down on the next note using left-hand fingering alone.

Fig. 6-10: Key signatures

Flat Keys

Sharp Keys

F

G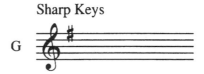

B♭

D

E♭

A

A♭

E

D♭

B

G♭

F♯

Two Practice Songs

After you're familiar with the material in this chapter—rereading it once, or twice, wouldn't be a bad idea—try to play the following two tunes.

Fig. 6-11: Polly Wolly Doodle

Fig. 6-12: **Drunken Sailor**

count: 1   2 + 3   4 +   1   2   3   4

seven

Mastering More Right-Hand Techniques

IN THIS CHAPTER, you'll explore some of the possibilities of playing the guitar by concentrating on what the right hand does. Right-hand technique is a major element in defining the difference in style between genres such as folk, country, and rock and roll.

Basic Rhythm Guitar

Up until now you've probably just been playing downstrokes. You've determined how many beats in the bar to count based on the time signature (4/4, 3/4, etc.). Now let's do some strumming or rhythm exercises using a pick. In this way, you will explore the possibilities of accents and different rhythms.

You should use a metronome for these exercises. Pick any chord—an E chord, for instance—and try these exercises. Try to keep time so well with the metronome that the sound of the "tick" disappears. You should make your time and chord changes as fluid as possible and as close to the metronome ticks as possible. Good time is more important here than good articulation. That will come with practice. If it helps, change between an E and an Ami chord every time there is an accent to play.

Now let's work on some rhythm guitar and accents. Try this exercise to develop your rhythm guitar playing:

Fig. 7-1

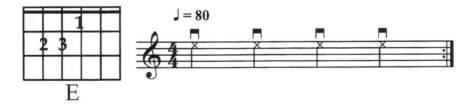

Fig. 7-2: Rhythm exercises

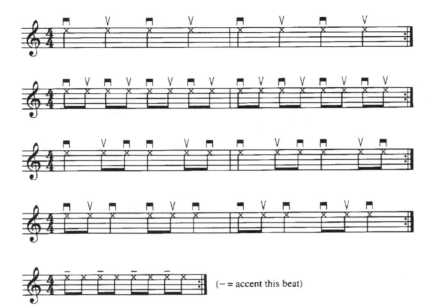

(− = accent this beat)

(With all these exercises, vary the upstrokes and the downstrokes.)

count: 1 + 2 + 3 + 4 +

Basic Alternate Bass Picking

Play an E chord. Play String 6 open with your pick, and then strum the rest of the chord using a downstroke, like this:

Fig. 7-3

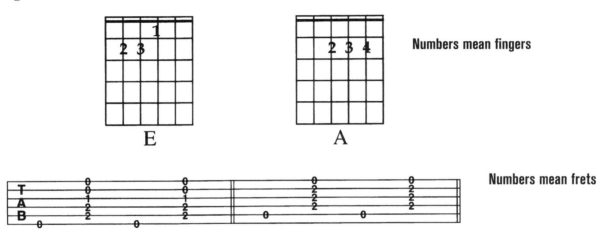

Numbers mean fingers

Numbers mean frets

This "boom-chick" kind of sound is called *alternating bass*. Playing the bass note on String 6 for the E chord and then the bass note on String 5 for the A chord starts to develop a pattern.

Eventually, you can really develop long bass note runs this way, suggesting a bass player accompanying the guitar, or the idea that you are playing left and right hands on a piano. To begin with, keep things very simple, with one bass note per chord. The coordination needed to play like this and sing along is really hard, so don't get upset if it all falls apart the first few times you try this.

Fig. 7-4: Wabash Cannonball

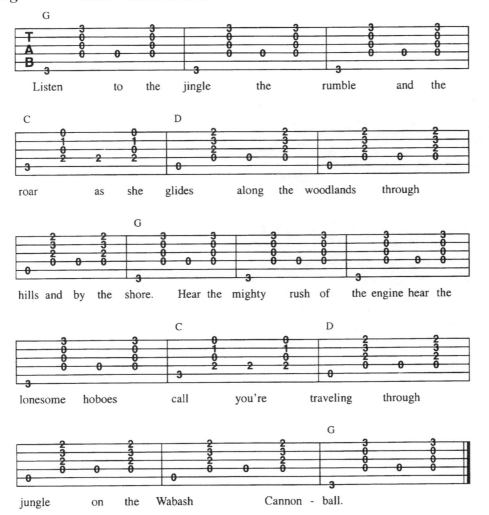

Basic Fingerpicking

The classical right-hand position and the folk and blues style right-hand positions are not identical, but the essence of the right-hand styles is the same.

Fig. 7-5: Right-hand position

The right-hand thumb plays the three bass strings, the first finger plays the third string, the second finger plays the second string, and the third finger plays the first string. The stroke comes from the finger joint, not the knuckle.

Fig. 7-6

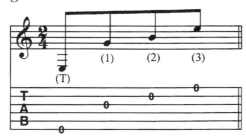

Fig. 7-7

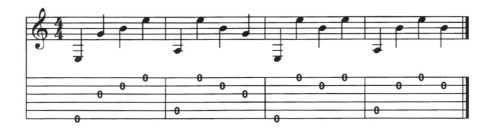

Fig. 7-7 continued

The difference between the hand position in folk/blues right-hand picking and classical guitar playing is one of degree. The folk/blues position seems more relaxed; it can also cause some muscle strain if you're not careful.

Go back and practice the early pick exercises using your fingers instead of the plectrum to play the treble strings.

Guitar Note

For a good classical technique, it's best to grow your nails slightly, so that you get a nice percussive attack, and slightly arch your wrist so that the fingers are vertical to the strings.

Folk Picking

Now that you have some basic ideas about how the right hand can work, let's explore some right-hand finger patterns used in various forms of music. We'll start with folk music. As you learn new songs, experiment with the different right-hand patterns shown in **Figure 7-8**.

Fig. 7-8

Pattern 1
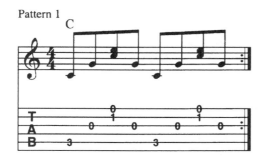

Pattern 2
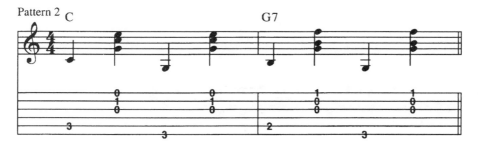

Pattern 3

Fig. 7-8 continued

Pattern 4

Pattern 5 "Carter Style"

(Play the notes with stems down with your thumb.)

Fig. 7-8 continued

Pattern 6 "Travis Style"

Step 1: Set up a bass pattern.

Step 2: Add a treble string, keeping the bass steady.

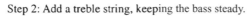

Step 3: Add a 2nd treble string, keeping the bass steady.

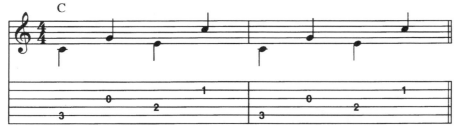

Fig. 7-8 continued

Step 4 (last step): Pinch the 1st string and 5th string together.

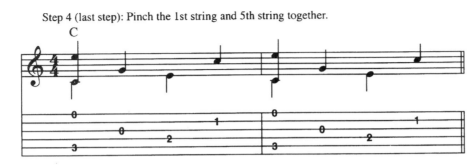

Notice that you use your thumb to play the bass notes. Also, pinch together a bass note and a treble string so that you can pick out the melody of a tune while giving the impression you're keeping a steady bass line going. This takes lots of practice but can sound really cool!

Basic Blues

The following illustration shows some basic blues rhythms to start you off.

Fig. 7-9

The next one shows a twelve-bar shuffle blues rhythm in tab form.

Fig. 7-10: 12-bar blues in A

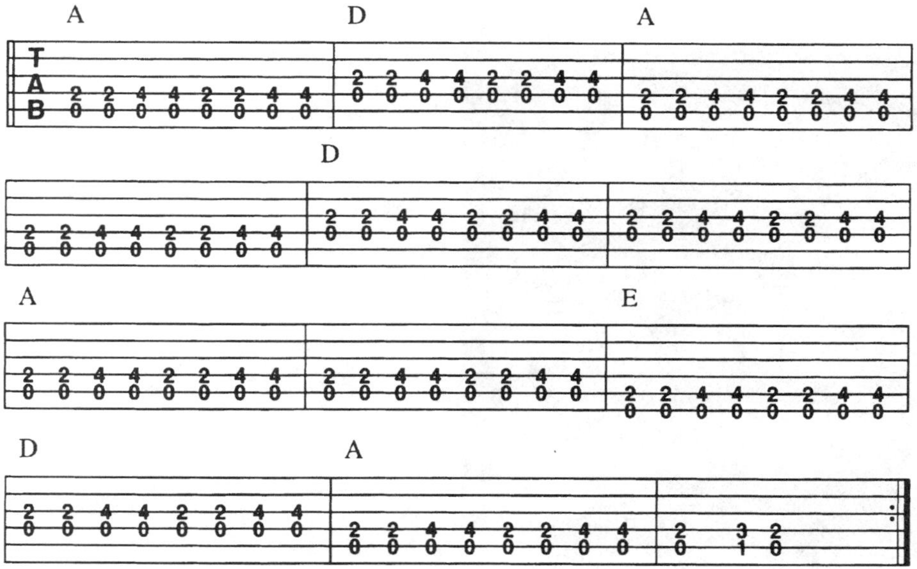

Country Picking

An advanced form of right-hand picking combines holding a pick and using the fingers at the same time.

Fig. 7-11

This type of picking is pretty hard to do, but is popular with country players and some jazz musicians who play solo guitar. Often it entails the unorthodox technique of using the little finger of the right hand, which is not used in any other fingerstyle technique.

eight

**Moving Beyond
Basics, and Moveable
Chord Shapes**

TO HELP YOU IMPROVE AS A GUITARIST beyond the very basics, in this chapter you'll learn a little more music theory, and some more types of chords. Don't worry if everything doesn't immediately come easily. Just go through the chapter again and keep working at it. It's clear that, if you've made it this far as a guitarist, you're in it for the long haul.

Adding to the Musical Alphabet

We discussed in Chapter 6 how the musical alphabet consists of seven letters: A-B-C-D-E-F-G. Actually, there are five other notes in the musical alphabet. Remember the flats and sharps we talked about at the end of Chapter 6? **Figure 8-1** shows how they are used to help represent the notes on the five black piano keys. (The numbers 1 through 6 at the bottom, by the way, are the notes played by strings on the guitar.)

Fig. 8-1:

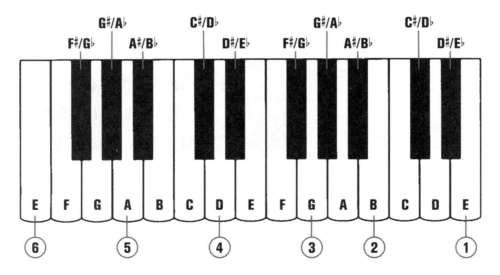

In Western music, musical notes move in half-steps. These half-steps correspond to the keys on a piano. The black keys represent the sharp/flat keys, and the white keys represent the notes without any sharps or flats.

Starting from E, there is a half-step between E and F. (This is the first pair of white notes that go together. We'll discuss this in the lesson on harmony.)

Between F and G there is a black note, which we can call either F# (F sharp), which is a half-step up from F, or G♭ (G flat), which is a half-step down from G.

♪ Guitar Note

Notice that at some points on the scale—represented by the black piano keys—the same note can be called either a sharp note or a flat note. F# and G♭, for example, are said to be *enharmonic notes*—that is, they're essentially the same note under a different name.

Between G and A there is another black note, called G# or A♭ for the same reason; similarly between A and B is a note called either A# or B♭.

Between B and C there is a half-step. (This is the second pair of white notes that go together.) Between C and D is C# or D♭; and between D and E is D# or E♭. Then we're back to E again.

The Chromatic Scale

All twelve notes together make up the musical alphabet and form what is called a *chromatic scale*. This is all you need to know to play and read music. As we've mentioned before, music is about what notes to play (melody), and how long you should play them (rhythm). The only other element you need to learn is harmony (which is what happens when you play two or more notes together at the same time). You'll more about this in Chapter 10.

Here is the complete chromatic scale moving in half-steps from the note E:

E, F, F#/G♭, G, G#/A♭, A, A#/B♭, B, C, C#/D♭, D, D#/E♭, (E).

This is how it looks written out in standard musical notation:

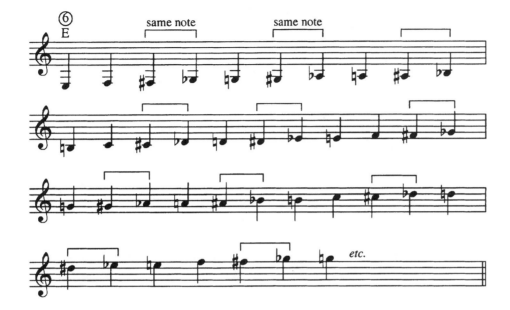

Fig. 8-2: The chromatic scale

Notice that in musical notation the sharp (♯) and flat (♭) signs come in front of the note. As mentioned earlier, a natural sign (♮) in front of a note means that you play that note without making it sharp or flat—as it is naturally played.

Scales on the Guitar

So how does the guitar fit into all this? You may recall that we said each fret of the guitar is a half-step away from the next. So the guitar fretboard naturally forms a chromatic scale.

If you play E, String 6, open, and then the note on every fret on the E string up to the twelfth fret, you will have played a chromatic scale starting on E. Try it.

If you play A, String 5, open, and then the note on every fret up to the twelfth fret, you will have played a chromatic scale starting on A, and so on. The next figure shows all the notes on all the strings.

Fig. 8-3

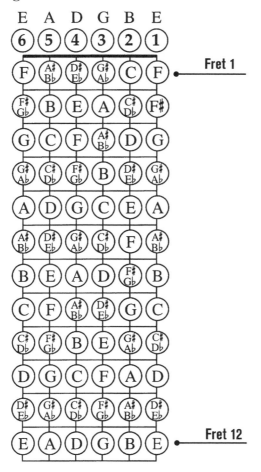

This is a really important concept, because now we can do lots of things on the guitar fretboard, not just confine ourselves to open-string chords. The most important thing we can do is move the same chord shape up and down the neck.

Playing Moveable Chords

The idea that we can move one shape up and down the neck and play lots of chords at the same time; these chords are called *moveable chords*.

You've already learned about major chords, minor chords, and seventh chords (also called dominant seventh chords). How did these different types of chords get their names? Why E, or C, or G7, or Ami? We'll go into this in more detail later. For now, all you need to know is that a chord has a name (or root) note. This note is usually found somewhere on one of the three bass strings.

For example, the name (root) note of E is on String 6, open.

Fig. 8-4

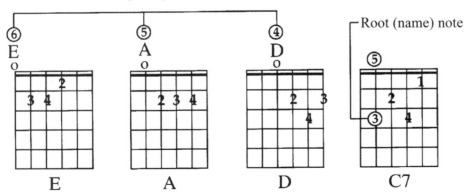

The name note or root note of A is found on String 5, open, and the name/root note of D is found on String 4, open.

The last chord in the previous figure is a new chord, called C7. It gets its name from the note on the third fret on String 5. When you play it, don't play String 6 or String 1; just play the inner four strings.

Using the same fingering, move that chord shape up two frets. Your third finger, on String 5, should now be at the fifth fret, and your first finger should be on String 2 at the third fret. (The other two fingers should be in the same pattern as the diagram, obviously.)

Remember, this chord gets its name from the note on String 5. Look at the chromatic scale, look at your fingers on the fretboard, and try to figure out what the name of this chord should now be. The question is: What's the name of the note on String 5 at the fifth fret?

Moving a C7 chord shape from the first position (your first finger is playing a note on the first fret, get it?) to the third position (first finger is now playing a note on the third fret) means that the new chord is called D7.

You may remember that back in Chapter 5 you were told a different way to play a D7 chord. That's absolutely true. In fact, you can play the same chord in different ways all over the guitar neck. Try this: Play the D7 chord as you originally learned it. Now play it using the new shape you've just learned. It's the same chord, but somehow it sounds subtly different. So you now have a choice of ways to play D7, depending on how the chord sounds. With a little practice, you'll find it's much easier to change from chord to chord using moveable shapes.

Barre Chords

Barre (pronounced *bar*) chords are a special kind of moveable chord. You create them by using your first finger to stop all the strings across a fret, and then you play a moveable shape under it. It's pretty easy, but it does take a little practice.

Practice this: Put your first finger across all six strings at the first fret. If you have trouble getting all the notes to sound clearly, put your second finger on top of your first to help press it down until the notes ring clearly. Relax. Flex your fingers. Now try it again. Move your first finger to the second fret, play the strings, then relax your hand. Repeat this at the third fret, and then the fourth—and so on—trying to get a clear sound from each note on the strings as you do it. Use that first finger to stop all the frets in turn as far up the neck as you can go, playing all the strings at a fret, relaxing your hand, and then trying again, all the time making sure that the notes on each string sound clear, and don't buzz or sound muffled.

Now look at the notes on String 6. If the root note, or name note, for the E major chord is String 6, open, then theoretically, if we move the "E shape" up one fret, we move the root note up one fret as well.

Use your first finger to bar the strings on the first fret. Use the suggested fingering to play an "E shape" chord at the first position/fret while you bar the first fret with your first finger. This is not easy, but persevere. Try to get all the notes on all the strings to sound clear when you play them. Relax your hand.

The note on the first fret of String 6 is F. That means that an "E shape" chord, which in the open-string position is called E, in the first position (that is, at the first fret) is called F. Move it up to the third fret and now it is called G.

Moveable Chords by Type

Figure 8-5 shows moveable chord types gathered together based on the location of the root note. Some of these chords have fingerings that are not that easy because they involve using more than one finger to bar more than one fret—A, for instance, or Dmi7—but with a little practice, you'll get it.

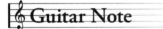 Guitar Note

A quick test: Try to find and play these chords:

G♭ (Major), F7, C#7, A♭, E♭7, and F#. (Hint: You'll find the root notes of all these chords on either String 6 or String 5.)

Fig. 8-5: E Shape: Major, Maj

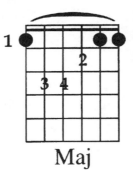

Maj

E Shape: dominant 7, 7, dom7

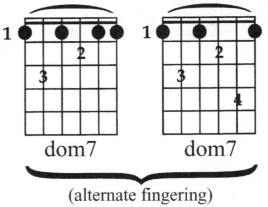

dom7   dom7

(alternate fingering)

E Shape: minor, mi

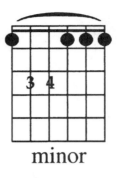

minor

E Shape: minor7, mi7

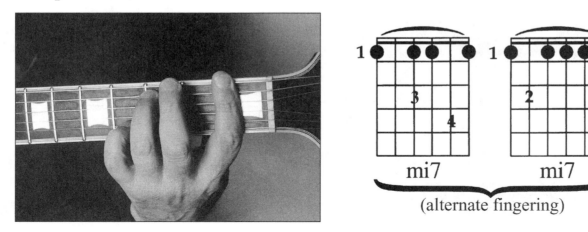

mi7   mi7

(alternate fingering)

A Shape: Maj (double barred chord)

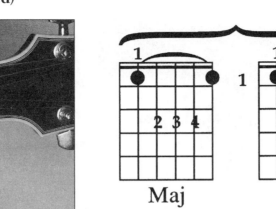

Maj   Maj

A Shape: dom7

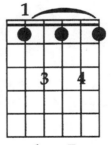

dom7

A Shape: Minor

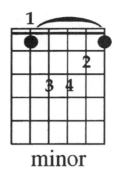

minor

A Shape: mi7

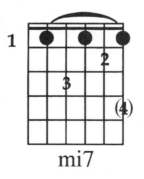

mi7

D Shape: Maj

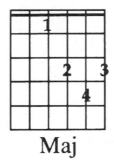

Maj

D Shape: dom7

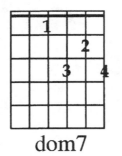

dom7

D Shape: mi

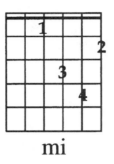

mi

D Shape: mi7

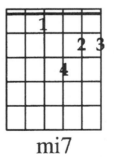

mi7

C Shape: Maj (half barre)

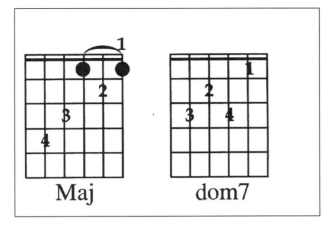

Maj   dom7

Moveable Chords with Muted Notes

Up until now we haven't discussed much about which strings you strum when you finger a chord. It's been enough that you get the strings to sound out clearly without buzzing or making some other noise while you fret the notes and play.

Earlier in this chapter, you were asked to play a C7 chord, and not to play String 6 and String 1, just the middle four strings. What that did, in a way, is mute or deaden the sound of String 6 and String 1 so that they wouldn't sound when you played the chord. That's because while the open note E is part of a C7 chord, if you move that chord shape up the neck, the note E quickly clashes with the other "C7 shape" chords that you play that don't contain the note E in them. (You'll learn more about why this is important in the lesson on harmony in Chapter 10.)

A *muted chord* is one in which you must deaden (or mute) one or two strings while you play the chord. You mute the strings so that you get the correct key tones out of the chord shape every time you play it, wherever you play it.

Fig. 8-6: A muted chord

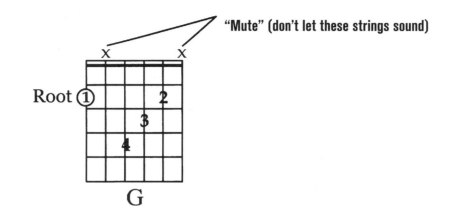

"Mute" (don't let these strings sound)

Root ①

G

This figure shows a moveable G chord with two strings (that is, notes) crossed out with an *x*: String 5 and String 1. That means you shouldn't let these strings sound when you play the chord. To mute a string, you need to shape your hand in such a way that these two strings are dampened or deadened when you strum a down-stroke. To sound the note, you've been told to use the tip of your finger on your left hand. To dampen or mute a note, use the "fatty" or flat part of either the side of your finger or just under your fingertip, depending on the kind of chord you're trying to play. Now play each of the remaining notes of the chord until they sound clear. Play them individually (called an arpeggio) to make sure you have them right.

We don't have the room here to fully explore this whole concept of moveable chords and muted chords. Now that you have an idea of how this works, you may want to pursue it further if it's something that appeals to you.

 nine

Playing
in Position

THINK ABOUT HOW FAR YOU'VE COME: It was only eight (not very long) chapters ago that we were discussing just what all those parts of the guitar were called. By the time you've mastered the concept of moveable chords and the material in this chapter, playing in position, you'll be able to think of yourself as an intermediate player.

The Basics of Position Playing

Up until now we've pretty much covered the basic things you can do using the open strings, or as it is more accurately called, in the open position. The simplest way to think of position playing is to think about where your first finger lies on the guitar neck. We talked about left-hand fingering in Chapter 5. You tried an exercise in which each finger of the left hand had a fret it covered. The first finger played notes on the first fret, the second finger played notes on the second fret, the third finger played notes on the third fret, and the fourth finger played notes on the fourth fret.

Strictly speaking, to play a chromatic scale we should only play three notes on String 3 because the fourth fret (B) is the same note as String 2, open (B), and there's no need to repeat. So try the chromatic scale again using the proper fingering.

Fig. 9-1: Chromatic scale fingering

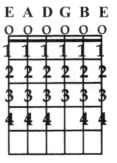

Using the open strings, we are playing in the open position. If we start this exercise on F (first fret String 6) and play it as shown in the following figure, then we are playing in the first position, because that is where the first finger is lying on the guitar fretboard.

Fig. 9-2: 1st position chromatic scale

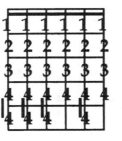

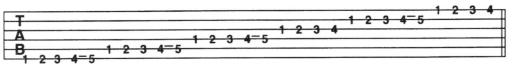

(Note: Slide your 4th finger up 1 fret to play the notes on the 5th fret.)

The idea of position playing changes how we look at the guitar fretboard. Up until now, we've been thinking about moving around the guitar fingerboard as going up and down the neck vertically—say from the first fret to the second, third, fourth, and so on—moving chord shapes from one fret to another in order to get different chords. The problem here is that you can end up jumping all over the neck trying to play two chords or notes one after the other. There ought to be a more efficient way of doing things—and there is.

Fig. 9-3

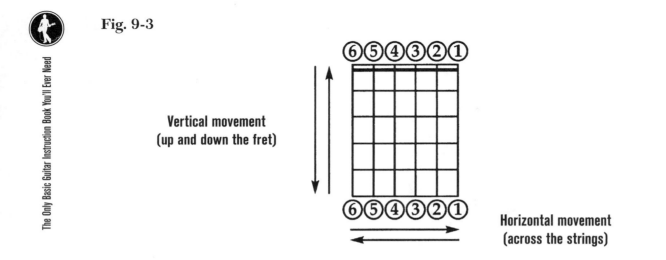

Vertical movement
(up and down the fret)

Horizontal movement
(across the strings)

In position playing, we're starting to think about playing within the same number of frets but moving horizontally across the fingerboard—that is, from String 6 to String 1) so your fingers aren't jumping all over the neck looking for notes and chords. This is another really important concept.

Playing a Scale

Let's move to the second position. That means the first finger will play all the notes on the second fret, and the other fingers will play the next four frets (second finger plays third fret, third finger plays fourth fret, fourth finger plays fifth fret).

Let's play a C major scale in position. Look at the next figure. Notice the fingering. Even though the first note C is played on the third fret with the second finger, we're still in the second position because of where the first finger is.

Fig. 9-4: C major scale in 2nd position

Now get really adventurous and play in the seventh position. (Remember, that means the first finger covers notes on the seventh fret.)

Guitar Note

One of the great things about playing in position is that it becomes much easier to read music. It may seem that the easiest place to read music on the guitar is in the open position, but really, only the first four notes on String 6 have to be played in this position. Everything else can be played somewhere else.

Look at the following figure and play the scale.

Fig. 9-5

VII ⑥

Notice that the Roman numeral VII means the VII fret (7th fret).

Fig. 9-6

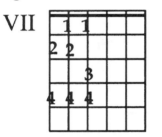

VII

Didn't you just play that? Yes, it's the C major scale, this time starting on String 6 at the eighth fret. But wait a second—the finger pattern was the same as in the second position.

However, you can also extend the scale and play it again (making two octaves). Look at the fingering of the next figure.

Fig. 9-7

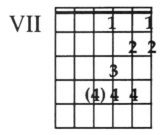

VII

Moveable Patterns

That's the trick about position playing. Because you aren't using open strings, you can really concentrate on a pattern of fingering and then move that pattern around the fingerboard, producing predictable results. If you learn, for example, that the fingering pattern for a major scale is 2–4, 1–2–4, 1–3–4, then you can play any major scale you like on String 6 and String 5. All you need to know is the name of the starting note.

If we play in the second position we can easily play the notes E, F, Gb, G, and Ab on String 6, but we can only play up to the note A on String 1, fifth fret, comfortably. That means if you have to read a piece of music that doesn't have a note higher than this range, the best place to play the music would be in the second position.

Fig. 9-8

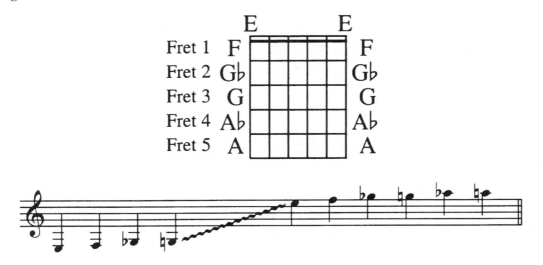

Look at "Daisy, Daisy." You can see that the highest note you have to play is A on the fifth fret, String 1, while the lowest note is A on String 5, open. So we can play the piece in the second position.

Fig. 9-9: Daisy, Daisy

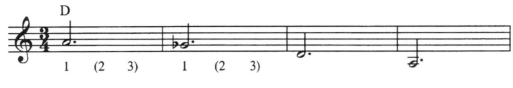

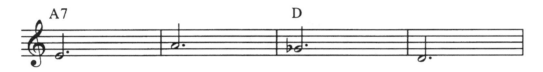

Fig. 9-9: Daisy, Daisy continued

Now let's try playing in the seventh position. It's really easy. The only notes you haven't learned yet are the notes on String 1 starting on the fifth fret—A, B♭, B, C, D♭, D.

Fig. 9-10

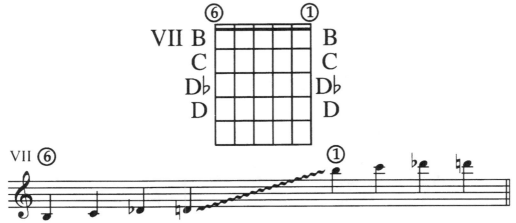

Here's the written range.

123

Now try the next exercise.

Fig. 9-11: 7th position exercise

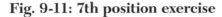

Of course, music doesn't have to be played in just one position—and it really shouldn't be. Very often we start in one position and then shift to another position, using what is called a position shift. Basically, all this means is that you move your first finger to a new place on the neck and the other fingers just naturally follow along.

Key Centers

You learned earlier that when we move the position of a chord, it becomes a different chord. For example, if we move an "E shape" chord to the fifth fret (fifth position), we're really playing an A chord. We can take that idea a little further here, by thinking of the fourth and fifth position as a good place to play chords, improvise solos, and so forth in the key of A. You'll need to experiment with this idea, but it really works. (Move one fret higher and suddenly you are playing in the key of Bb.)

Similarly, you can play in the key of G at the second and third positions, or the key of C at the seventh and eighth positions. It also means that unusual keys like Bb, F#, Db, or B are really exactly the same as G or C or D, they're just at a different fret position. With a minimum of effort, you can suddenly play in any key, as long as you know the best position in which to play the key. Just remember, the first finger is the guide to moving the hand around the fingerboard, either vertically or horizontally.

124

ten

Learning
Basic Harmony

THE SAME THREE IDEAS are the basis of all the music you've ever heard: melody, rhythm, and harmony. You've learned quite a lot about melody and rhythm; now we'll look at the third element, harmony, which is what happens when you play two or more notes together at the same time.

The Rules of Harmony

Most people expect music to sound a certain way, and as a result there are "rules" about how, when, and why certain notes should go together. Even if you're into extremely experimental music, to really stretch the envelope it's best that you have some understanding of the rules you're about to break.

What we are going to look at applies equally to all the keys—to any key, in fact. But to make it easier to understand, we're going to look at everything in the key of C. The key of C does not naturally have any sharps or flats (accidentals), so the variations and so forth can be more easily seen.

Here is the scale of C major. Notice that the notes fall alternately on lines and spaces. For example, C is on a ledger line, D is on a space, E is on a line, F is on a space, and so on.

Fig. 10-1: C major scale

THE SAME THREE IDEAS

Understanding Intervals

Let's start with the concept of the distance between two notes, which is called an interval. You'll remember that the frets of a guitar are a half-step (sometimes called a halftone) apart. A halftone (also called a semitone) is the smallest interval, or distance, between two notes—at least in Western music. This is the distance from C to C#. (C# is one half-step up from C, remember, and D♭ is enharmonically the same note, a half-step down from D.)

A whole step or whole tone (usually just called a tone), which is two semitones, would be from C to D. This would be the equivalent of jumping to a note two frets away on the guitar. Let's apply this to the guitar. Look at the fingerboard.

The distance from C, third fret, String 5 to C#, fourth fret, String 5 is a semitone.

The distance from C, third fret, String 5 to D, fifth fret, String 5 is a whole tone.

From C to D♭ is a minor second—that is, one semitone.

From C to D is a second—that is, two semitones.

From C to E♭ is a minor third—three semitones.

From C to E is a major third—four semitones.

From C to F is a fourth—five semitones.

From C to G♭ is a diminished or flattened fifth—six semitones. If we say the interval is from C to F# (enharmonically the same note as G♭, remember), this can be called an augmented fourth. Flattening—or diminishing—a note means dropping it down a semitone or fret. Augmenting a note means sharpening or raising it a semitone or fret.

From C to G is a fifth—seven semitones.

From C to G# is an augmented fifth (also called a raised fifth)—eight semitones. In the same way as before, C to A♭ (enharmonically the same note) is a minor sixth.

From C to A is a major sixth—nine semitones.

From C to A# is an augmented sixth—ten semitones. In the same way, from C to B♭ is a minor seventh—ten semitones.

From C to B is a major seventh—eleven semitones.

From C to C is an octave—twelve semitones.

Fig. 10-2: Intervals written in notation

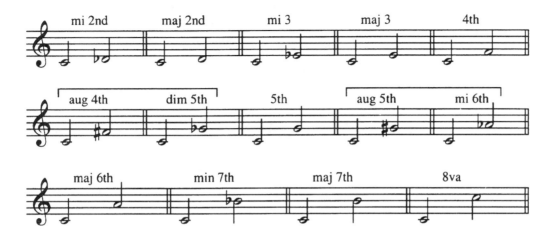

Building Scales

Both major scales and minor scales are created by putting together a series of tones and semitones. Of course, depending on whether the scale is major or minor, these tones and semitones are arranged in a different sequence.

Major Scales

Both major scales and minor scales are created by putting together a series of tones and semitones. Of course, depending on whether the scale is major or minor, these tones and semitones are arranged in a different sequence.

If we look at the major scale again, we can see it is built this way:

C to D—tone

D to E—tone

E to F—semitone
F to G—tone
G to A—tone
A to B—tone
B to C—semitone

So the pattern for a major scale is tone, tone, semitone, tone, tone, tone, semitone.

Minor Scales

Each major scale has a corresponding minor scale (called the *relative minor*), built on the sixth note of the major scale. There are three different types of minor scales that we can study: the harmonic minor, the melodic minor, and the natural minor. Each scale is built slightly differently from the other.

The natural minor scale is the easiest to start with because it's composed of all the notes of the related major scale (in this case, C), starting on the sixth note of the scale.

Fig. 10-3

C Major Scale

A Natural Minor Scale
(starts on 6th of C scale)

A harmonic minor scale consists of tone, semitone, tone, tone, semitone, minor third, semitone.

Fig. 10-4

A Harmonic Minor Scale

C Harmonic Minor Scale

In the key of A minor, it would be called A harmonic minor:

A to B—tone
B to C—semitone
C to D—tone
D to E—tone
E to F—semitone
F to G#   mi—third
G# to A—semitone

In the key of C it would be C harmonic minor, and would be built this way: C-D-E♭-F-G-A♭-B-C.

A melodic minor scale is more complex because it is often played in classical harmony as ascending in one form and descending in another. However, for our purposes we'll learn it the same way going up and down.

The melodic minor is built of tone, semitone, tone, tone, tone, tone, semitone. In the key of A melodic minor it would be A-B-C-D-E-F#-G#-A.

In the key of C melodic minor it would be C-D-E♭-F-G-A-B-C.

Fig. 10-5

A Melodic Minor Scale

C Melodic Minor Scale

Understanding Chord Structures

The combination of three or more notes is a chord. Three note chords are called *triads*. Four note chords are called *seventh chords*.

Triads

There are four types of triads: major, minor, augmented, and diminished, which are built by piling major thirds and minor thirds on top of each other in different combinations. You can "spell" the four triad chords this way:

C maj	C-E-G	maj 3rd min 3rd
C mi	C-E♭-G	min 3rd maj 3rd
C aug	C-E-G#	maj 3rd maj 3rd
C dim	C-E♭-G♭	mi 3rd mi 3rd

Most chord structures are a variation on these four triads.
The following figure gives you an example of how these triads can be played on the guitar.

Fig. 10-6

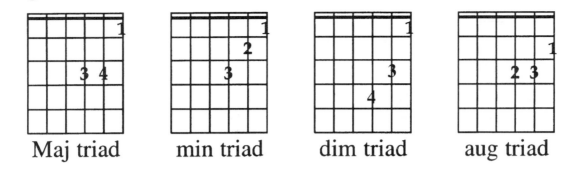

Maj triad   min triad   dim triad   aug triad

On the guitar, these simple chords are not usually spelled this way. For example, you can mix up the order of the notes, and instead of playing C-E-G, you can play G-C-E. You can also double notes. An E maj triad is spelled E-G#-B, for example, but it is usually played E-B-E-G#-B-E.

Seventh Chords

Four-note chords are called seventh chords. They generally have much more color and sound more interesting than triads. Furthermore, they are the basis of all our standard repertoire of tunes. To make a seventh chord, add either a major third or a minor third to one of the four triad forms. Doing this, we get five basic seventh chords, with other chords being variations on these five.

In the key of C, the five are:

C maj7	C-E-G-B	
C7	C-E-G-B♭	(also called a dominant 7)
C mi7	C-E♭-G-B♭	
C mi7♭5	C-E♭-G♭-B♭	(also written C⌀7 or C half diminished)
C dim7	C-E♭-G♭-A	(usually called B double flat, but we'll call it A, which enharmonically it is)

Guitar Note

It's not really important right now to know all these structures inside out. Instead, learn the chord forms on the chord diagrams. Try to figure out where other triads can be played on the guitar and write them down for yourself.

As you've seen, we can make chords up by piling thirds on top of each other. Another way to look at chords is to build them from the tones of a scale (major or minor—it doesn't matter).

Here's a C major scale again:	C	D	E	F	G	A	B	C
Putting underneath:	1	2	3	4	5	6	7	8
Now using Roman numerals:	I	II	III	IV	V	VI	VII	VIII

A chord can be built by choosing every other note in the scale and then altering it if necessary:

Cmaj7	1-3-5-7
C7	1-3-5-♭7
Cmi7	1-♭3-5-♭7
Cmi7♭5	1-♭3-♭5-♭7
Cdim	1-♭3-♭5-♭7

On the piano keyboard it is easier to play these chords as spelled out here, but on the guitar that isn't the case. A Cmaj7 chord, for example, is often played on the guitar spelled C-G-B-E, or C-B-E-G.

If you spend some time working on understanding how chords are built, you'll soon be able to build your own. For example, if you know how to play a Cmaj7 chord, and suddenly you are confronted with Cmaj7#5, you just need to play a Cmaj7 shape, figure out which note is the fifth of the chord, and raise it up a fret (semitone) to make the #5 part of this chord. (The chord, of course, would be spelled 1-3-#5-7—that is, in the key of C: C-E-G#-B.)

You read earlier that there are five basic seventh chords. That's true, but there are seven more chords that are variations on these five. Here are the twelve:

Cmaj7	1-3-5-7
C7	1-3-5-♭7
Cmi7	1-♭3-5-♭7
Cmi7♭5	1-♭3-♭5-♭7
Cdim7	1-♭3-♭5-♭7(6)
Cmaj7#5	1-3-#5-7
Cmaj7♭5	1-3-♭5-7
C7#5	1-3-#5-♭7
C7♭5	1-3-♭5-♭7
Cmimaj7	1-♭3-5-7 (C minor major 7)
C6	1-3-5-6
Cmi6	1-♭3-5-6

Think about this: a mi6 chord, and a mi7♭5 chord are the same thing, although they will have different root notes: Cmi6 = Ami7♭5.

Arpeggios

An arpeggio is simply a "broken" chord. In other words, if you play individually the notes that make up a chord—say Cmaj7 (C-E-G-B)—you are playing a Cmaj7 arpeggio. To play these arpeggios properly, you should learn them in two octaves. For example, C-E-G-B-C, E-G-B-C.

Single-note arpeggio practice (meaning playing one note of a chord at a time) is a wonderful way of getting these sounds in your head. It's also a terrific basis for learning how to improvise over a chord sequence.

Diatonic Chords

If you go through a major scale, building chords on every note of the scale by using every other note, you get what we call diatonic chords—all the chords that naturally occur in the key.

In the key of C, these are Cmaj7, Dmi7, Emi7, Fmaj7, G7, Ami7, Bmi7♭5, Cmaj7.
If you go through a harmonic minor scale, you get this sequence:
CmiMaj7, Dmi7♭5, E♭maj7#5, Fmi7, G7, A♭maj7, Bdim7, CmiMaj7.

Standard Progressions

Standard, in this case, means "generally accepted" or "normal." There are standard tunes like "Over the Rainbow" and even "Happy Birthday to You" that are created using certain chord progressions, which means that a chord naturally progresses to another chord after it's played. (A G7 chord, for example, naturally progresses to a Cmaj7, partly because G is the fifth note in the scale and key of C.)

If you go back and look at the seventh chords in the key of C, each has a Roman numeral under it. There's a reason for this. Instead of saying Cmaj7-Fmaj7-G7, for example, we could just say I IV V. Then we could look at the notes of any major scale, and play the I IV and V chords built on the first, fourth, and fifth notes of the scale. (They would be a maj7, maj7, dom7 sequence of chords.)

The Cycle of Fourths and Fifths

If you go back to Chapter 6 and look at the section on key signatures, you may notice something now. If you follow the key signatures carefully, you'll see that from C to F is a fourth, and from F to B♭ is a fourth, and so on through the flat keys. Similarly, C to G is a fifth, G to D is a fifth, D to A is a fifth, and so on through the sharp keys. In fact, a fourth in one direction is a fifth in the other.

Fig. 10-7

Cycle of 4th and 5ths

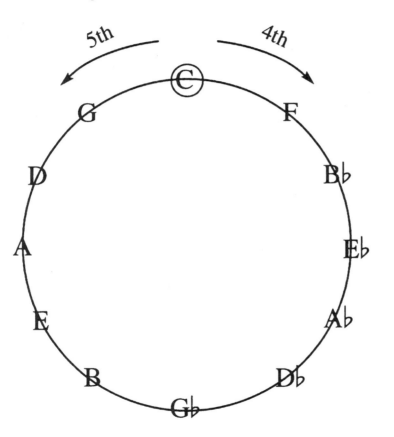

You've seen that we can use Roman numerals instead of chords. Following the flat keys (the notes that are a fourth away from each other), we get a series of V I chords. That is, C7 resolves to Fmaj7; F7 resolves to B♭maj7; B♭7 resolves to E♭maj7; E♭7 resolves to A♭maj7; A♭7 resolves to D♭maj7; D♭7 resolves to G♭maj7; G♭7 resolves to Bmaj7; B7 resolves to Emaj7; E7 resolves to Amaj7; A7 resolves to Dmaj7; D7 resolves to Gmaj7; and G7 resolves to C.

The Blues

Finally, let's consider a fun and usable progression to look at the blues. A blues sequence is really just a I IV V sequence. So a blues in B♭, say, would be B♭maj7, E♭maj7, F7.

Here's a basic twelve-bar blues in C (using triads):

```
4/4  C / / / | F / / / | C / / / |       |
     F / / / |         | C / / / |       |
     G / / / |         | C / / / |      ||
```

This is kind of bland, so let's use dominant seven chords.

```
4/4 C7 / / / | F7 / / / | C7 / / / |       |
    F7 / / / |          | C7 / / / |       |
    G7 / / / |          | C7 / / / |      ||
```

A slightly more complicated sequence is called I VI II V. This sequence is the basis of most standard tune chord progressions. Using the diatonic chords you learned about earlier, in the key of C this would be Cmaj7, Ami7, Dmi7, G7. If you analyze songs by figuring out their key signatures, you'll discover that this I IV II V sequence is used in a lot of them.

One of the things you may well discover is that the root notes in the VI II V I sequence are all a fourth apart. (In key of C: A to D to G to C.) Next time you play a song, look for this pattern and this sequence. The more you practice using this cycle of fourths, the easier playing standard song progressions becomes.

Try this jazzy blues sequence:

4/4 C7 / / / | F7 / F#dim7 / | C7 / / / | Gmi7 / C7 / |
     F7 / / / | F#dim7 / / / |C7/ / / | A7#5 / / / |
     Dm7 / / / | G7 / / / |C7 / / / | (G7#5 / / /) ||

When you practice chords and scales, try to practice them in the cycle of fourths sequence. First, play a C major scale, then an F major scale, then a B♭ major scale, and so on.

Appendix One

Glossary

accent: A dynamic effect that places an emphasis on a note or chord.

accidentals: Symbols in written music to raise (# - sharpen) or lower (♭ - flatten) notes by semitones. A double flat (♭♭) lowers the pitch by a tone. A natural (♮) cancels the accidental alteration.

acoustic guitar: A hollow-bodied guitar that does not require electronic amplification.

action: The strings' playability along the neck. Action is affected by the strings' distance from the neck, the neck straightness, and the string gauge.

altered chord: A chord or scale in which one or more of the notes is changed to a note not normally associated with that scale.

archtop: A guitar, often an acoustic, with a curved top (soundboard) and F-holes similar to a violin's.

arpeggio: Literally, "like a harp"—that is, playing the notes of a chord one after the other rather than together. Also known as a broken chord.

artificial harmonics: Harmonics produced by fingering a note on the frets and lightly touching the string a fourth higher.

atonal: Not part of the tonal system of major and minor keys; in no key at all.

augmented (see also diminished): Intervals increased by a semitone are known as *augmented intervals*. The augmented chord is a major chord with the fifth raised a semitone.

bebop, hard bop: A style of jazz that emerged in the 1940s, using fast melodic lines over adventurous extended harmonies, The terms *bop* and *bebop* are interchangeable, and *hard bop* usually refers to the 1950s blues-influenced variant.

binding: Thin strips of wood or plastic that seal the edges of the body.

blues: An African-American style of music that uses a scale including flattened thirds, fifths, and sevenths, known as the "blue notes" in a scale. A blues style has a predominantly twelve-bar form.

body: The main part of the guitar, to which the bridge and neck are attached. On acoustic guitars and some electrics, the body serves as a resonating chamber.

boogie-woogie: A style of blues and jazz with a repetitive rhythmic bass figure derived from early jazz piano-playing.

bossa nova: A Brazilian rhythmic style of jazz and popular music widespread in the United States and Europe in the 1960s.

bottleneck guitar: A technique using a metal bar or tube rather than the fingers of the left hand to play notes and chords, and to slide from one to another.

braces: Interior wooden strips that strengthen a hollow-bodied guitar. Brace size and configuration partly determine a guitar's tone.

break: In jazz, a short solo passage without accompaniment that usually occurs at the end of a phrase.

bridge: The structure that holds the saddle (or saddles), over which strings pass on the guitar body. Most bridges can be adjusted to raise or lower string height, changing the guitar's action and intonation.

capo: A spring-loaded, adjustable clamp that becomes in effect a "moveable nut." It fits over the neck and covers all the strings at a given fret, raising the pitch of the strings and allowing a singer or flamenco player to play in a different key and still use open-string chords and fingering.

chamber music: Music for small groups of players (usually no more than nine). The term *chamber jazz* is sometimes used for the more formal style of small combo such as the Modern Jazz Quartet.

changes: The sequence of chords used as a basis for improvisation in jazz.

choking: Damping the strings of the guitar to give short staccato chords.

chords: Any combination of three notes played together, usually based on the triad formed by the first, third, and fifth notes of the scale. For example, the chord of C major consists of C (the root of the chord), F, and G. Chords can be in root position—that is, with the root as the bass note—or various inversions using other notes in the chord as the bass.

chord substitutions: In jazz, alternatives to the conventionally used chords in a sequence.

chorus: On an electric guitar, simulates the effect of more than one instrument playing the same note.

chromatic: Chromatic notes are those that fall outside the notes of the key a piece of music is in. The chromatic scale is a twelve-note scale moving in semitones.

classical: The term *classical* is used loosely to describe art music to distinguish it from folk, jazz, rock, pop, and so forth, but more precisely it refers to the period of music from around 1750 through 1830.

comping: Jazz jargon for *accompanying*.

compression: On an electric guitar, boosts the volume of quieter notes, and reduces that of louder ones, evening out the sound of fast passages.

counterpoint, contrapuntal: The playing of two or more tunes at the same time, within the same harmonic framework. The added tunes are sometimes called *countermelodies*.

country (and western): A predominantly white, rural popular music originally from the Southern and Western United States.

cutaway: An indented area of the body that allows the guitarist's fretting hand to access notes higher up the neck.

delay (echo): On an electric guitar, mimics the echo effect by playing a delayed copy of the original sound.

detuning: Intentionally putting one or more of the strings out of tune for a specific effect.

diatonic: Using the notes of the major scale.

diminished: Intervals decreased in size by a semitone are known as *diminished intervals*. The diminished chord is based on intervals of a minor third, and the so-called diminished scale consists of alternating tones and semitones.

distortion: Change of tone quality, with a harsh sound, achieved by overdriving an amplifier, or the use of a distortion pedal, fuzz box, or overdriver.

double stopping: Forming a chord by stopping two or more strings with the left hand on the frets.

double or (multi) tracking: Recording technique enabling a player to superimpose a number of "takes" of a particular piece.

dreadnought: A large-bodied, steel-strung acoustic guitar.

drone strings: Strings not intended to be played with the fingers, but tuned to vibrate in sympathy with the main instrument's strings.

effects: Numerous special effects are possible on a modern electric guitar, including chorus, compression, delay, distortion, enhancer, expander, flanger, fuzz, harmonizer, Leslie, octave divider, overdrive, panning, preamp, reverb, tremolo, vibrato, volume pedal, and wah-wah (see separate listings for each).

enhancer: On an electric guitar, device to improve sound definition.

expander: The opposite of compressor, increasing the range of volume on an electric guitar.

F-holes: Violin-style F-shaped sound holes, usually found in pairs.

feedback: The loud whine produced by a microphone or pickup receiving and amplifying its own signal from a loudspeaker.

fill: In jazz and rock, a short melodic figure played by an accompanying instrument between phrases.

fingerpicking: Right-hand technique in which the strings are plucked by individual fingers.

Flamenco: A Spanish style of playing, singing, and dancing. Forms of flamenco include *alegrias, buierias, fandangos, farrucas, ganadinas, malaguena, seguidillas, siguiryas, soleas,* and *tarantas*, and the guitar often interjects *falsetas* (melodic improvised interludes) into these forms. Techniques in flamenco guitar-playing include *alzapua* (up-and-down strokes with the thumbnail), *apagado* (left-hand damping), *golpe* (tapping on the body of the guitar), *picado* (fingerstyle), and *rasqueado* (strumming by unfurling the fingers across the strings).

flanger: On an electric guitar, a chorus-type effect, using a delayed signal with a slight pitch variation.

flat-top: A guitar whose soundboard, or top, is flat.

fretboard: The wooden strip, usually of hardwood, attached atop the neck and into which the frets are set. Also called the *fingerboard*.

frets: Metal wires set into the fret-board at precise distances, allowing the strings to sound the correct pitches along the neck.

folk: The music of rural cultures, usually passed down orally. The word folk is also used to describe composed music in the style of true folk music, particularly after the "folk revival" of the 1950s.

free jazz: A jazz style of the 1960s, which is freely improvised without reference to a specific tune or harmonic sequence.

fusion: A jazz-rock fusion, but also any form of "crossover" from one style to another.

fuzz: On an electric guitar, a form of distortion, operated by a fuzz pedal.

gig bags: A portable padded bag made of either canvas, nylon, or leather that you can use as an alternative to a hard case. They zip shut and offer about the same protection as a piece of soft leather luggage.

glissando: A slide from one note to another.

grace notes: Short notes played just before the main note of a tune as an ornament.

groove: A repeated rhythmic pattern in jazz and rock

guitar synthesizer: Guitars with built-in synthesizers for dramatically altering the sound, or equipped with MIDI to control external synthesizers, drum machines, and so on.

habañera: A Cuban dance, or its rhythm.

hammer-on: Notes played by hammering the string with the fingers of the left hand, rather than plucking with the right hand.

harmonics: Notes with an ethereal tone higher than the pitch of the string, produced by lightly touching the string at certain points.

harmonizer: On an electric guitar, a chorus-type effect adding a sound in harmony with the original signal.

head: In jazz, the statement of the tune before and after the improvised solos.

headstock: The structure at the end of the neck that holds the tuning machines.

interval: The distance between two notes. For example, C to G is a fifth (that is, five notes of the scale); C to E is a third (three notes); and C to C is an octave (eight notes).

inversion: see *chords*.

jazz: African-American in origin, characterized by the use of improvisation, "blue notes," and syncopated rhythms.

Latin: Music of Latin-American origin, including dance rhythms such as the *habañera*, samba, rumba, bossa nova, and so on.

legato: Smoothly, not staccato.

Leslie: The Leslie cabinet, originally for use with electronic organs, contains a rotating speaker, giving a swirling effect to music played on an electric guitar.

licks: In jazz and rock, short, almost clichéd, phrases inserted into a solo or used as rills.

machine head: See *tuning peg*.

microtone: Interval of less than a semitone.

MIDI: Musical Instrument Digital Interface. This allows musical instruments such as electric guitars and synthesizers to communicate with sequencers, effects boxes, computers, and so on.

minimalism: A movement in music from the 1960s using static harmonies, repeated patterns, and a minimum of material.

modes: Scales using the notes of the diatonic scale, other than the major and minor scales. The modes, such as Dorian, Phrygian, and Aeolian, originated in medieval music, but were adopted by jazz players in the 1950s.

modulate: Move from one key to another.

neck: The long structure that runs from the body to the headstock, and onto which the fretboard is attached. Necks have a longitudinal curve that can be adjusted by means of the truss rod. The width, shape, and curvature of the neck largely determine a guitar's playability.

nut: The notched fitting—usually of bone, ivory, ebony, metal, or plastic—that guides the strings from the fretboard to the tuning pegs.

octave divider: On an electric guitar, an early form of harmonizer, adding a sound an octave above or below the original signal.

open tuning: Tuning the strings of the guitar to a specific chord, rather than the conventional E-A-D-G-B-E. There are also other nonconventional tunings, such as D-A-D-G-A-D.

overdrive: On an electric guitar, a form of distortion.

overdubs: Parts added to a recording after the original take.

panning: On an electric guitar, moving the source of the sound within the stereo field.

partial chords: Chords not using all the strings of the guitar.

passing chords: Chords used "in passing" from one harmony to another, not part of the main harmonic sequence.

pedal note: A repeated bass note that supports a sequence of changing harmonies.

pentatonic: A scale of five, rather than the more usual seven, notes.

phasing: On an electric guitar, playing two identical sounds slightly out of phase with one another.

pick or plectrum: Object used for striking the guitar strings, usually made from plastic.

pickguard: A protective plate on the body of the guitar that protects the top from being scratched by a pick or fingers.

pickup: The device on electric guitars that picks up and transmits the sound of the strings to the amplifier.

pickup switch: Allows pickups to be turned on individually or in various combinations.

potentiometer (pot): A variable resistor used for an electric guitar's volume and tone controls. Amplifiers also have pots.

preamp: With an electric guitar, the preamplifier can be used as a form of tone control, or to boost the signal.

pull-off: A note played by pulling the string with the fingers of the left hand.

raga: A scale used in Indian music. There are hundreds of different ragas, many using microtones.

ragtime: An African-American style of music, a precursor of jazz.

reverb: On an electric guitar, this mimics the echo effect, either by a built-in spring reverb or a digital electronic emulation.

rhythm and blues: African-American pop music originating in the late 1940s, the precursor to rock-and-roll.

riff: In jazz and rock, a short, repeated melodic phrase.

rock, rock-and-roll: Rock evolved in the 1950s from rhythm and blues, and in its 1960s form became known simply as rock.

rubato: Not strictly in tempo—played freely and expressively.

rumba (rhumba): Afro-Cuban dance.

saddle: The fitting that guides the strings over the bridge. Most electric guitars have individual saddles for each string. These can be adjusted to change a string's length and thus intonation.

scales: A series of ascending or descending notes in a specific key, the basis for compositions in the tonal system.

segue: Moving without a break to the next movement, section, or number.

semitone: A half-step, or halftone. The smallest interval in the diatonic scale—for example, the distance between E and F, or B and C.

serial, twelve-tone: Avant-garde compositional method using the twelve notes of the chromatic scale in series, without reference to traditional harmony or tonality.

slide: A style of guitar-playing using bottleneck, where notes and chords slide from one to another.

solid-body: A guitar whose body is made from a solid piece of wood or is a solid lamination. Most electrics are solid bodies; some are semi-hollow.

soundboard: The resonating top of an acoustic guitar.

sound hole: A hole (or holes) in the top of a guitar through which sound is emitted.

staccato: Detached. Staccato notes or chords are short and clipped, not smoothly moving to the next.

straight eights: In jazz, playing *straight eights* means playing exactly on the beat, whereas *swing* indicates that the rhythm should be interpreted more freely. (See also *swing*.)

string-bending: Using the fingers of the left hand to pull a string to one side, "bending" the pitch of the note.

strings: The cords that are plucked to cause vibrations that produce a guitar's sound. Most guitar strings are solid wire or thin wire wrapped around a solid core; classical guitars have nylon and metal-wound nylon strings. A string's thickness (gauge) depends on its position on the guitar and the relative thickness of the entire six-string set.

swap fours: In jazz, when soloists alternate improvisations with one another every four bars.

swing: A style of jazz of the 1940s, mainly for big bands. Also an instruction to play rhythms freely. (See also straight eights.)

syncopation: Shifting the accent of a melody off the main beat of the bar—a characteristic of jazz and much rock and pop music.

tailpiece: The device that holds the strings' ball ends.

tempo: The underlying speed of a piece of music.

timbre: The tone quality of a sound.

tonal, tonality: Relating to the system of major and minor keys.

tone (whole tone): An interval of two semitones—for example, the distance between C and D, or F and G.

tremolo: On an electric guitar, small and rapid variation in the volume of a note. This effect is often confused with vibrato; the tremolo arm or bar is used to bend the pitch of notes on electric guitars.

trill: Rapid alternation between one note and the note above.

truss rod: A metal rod that runs lengthwise through the neck, increasing its strength and allowing adjustment of the longitudinal curve.

truss rod adjusting nut: The part of the truss rod system that can be tightened or loosened to alter rod tension.

tuning pegs: Devices set into the headstock that anchor strings and allow them to be tuned. Each tuning machine consists of a post, a geared mechanism, and a tuning key.

turnaround: In jazz, the harmony under the last phrase of a tune, taking the music back to the beginning for its repeat.

unison: On exactly the same note. For example, on a twelve-string guitar, the pairs of strings are tuned in unison—that is, to the same note. In jazz, the tune of the head is often played by several instruments in unison.

vamps, vamping: Repeated accompanying figure in jazz and popular music before the melody begins.

vibrato: On an electric guitar, small and rapid variation in the pitch of a note.

voicing: The spacing of the notes in a chord. .

volume pedal: Means of altering the volume of sound for an electric guitar, useful in creating the "fade-in" effect or as a "swell" pedal.

wah-wah: With an electric guitar, the wah-wah pedal controls the relative bass and treble response of a sound. Fully down it has a high treble tone; fully up it emphasizes the bass. The characteristic "wah-wah" sound is achieved by rocking the pedal back and forth.

whole-tone scale: A six-note augmented scale formed entirely of intervals of a whole tone, such as C-D-E-F#-G#-A#.

Appendix Two

Guitar Tricks

Hammer-On

This is used a lot in rock, blues, and folk playing. Fret a note with your first finger, say D at the fifth fret, String 5. Now, while the note is still ringing, "hammer down" your finger on E at the seventh fret, String 5, and keep it there.

Pull-Off

This is really a hammer-on in reverse. You need to have both fingers on the fret. Play the note E, as before, then pull off your finger so the D will sound clearly.

Trill

If you rapidly combine both techniques above, you get a trick often used in rock-and-roll that may sound familiar, called a trill.

String Bends

A lot of rock guitarists and blues guitarists use a string bend. If you pull or push the string, once you've fretted the note, you can actually bend it almost to the note on the next fret. It's the same sort of technique as using a mechanical tremolo arm. It generally works best if you use thin gauge strings.

Double String Bends

A rock and blues cliché, but effective on occasion if the spirit moves you. The trick is to have both fingers in place ahead of time. Here, you play the D, on the seventh fret of String 3, bending it until you've reached the pitch of E, and—while still sounding the bent note—play E on an adjacent string (fifth fret, String 2), letting the two notes ring together.

Another trick is to play the D and E together (major second), fingering them as above, and then bend the D into an E, letting the two Es sound together.

Vibrato

This just means deliberately invoking a "wow-wow" kind of effect. All you do is rock your finger back and forth on the note as you fret it. The more exaggerated the movement of your hand, the broader will be the "vib."

Slide

This is simple. Slide your finger from one fret to another while the note is still ringing.

Index